The Business of Possibility

Re-imagining your
organisation –
revealing the essence
of the entrepreneur

DEDICATION

To those who recognise that we best serve the common good when under the influence of our innate kindness, understanding, wisdom and common sense –
The Realm of Possibility

The Business *of* Possibility

Re-imagining your
organisation –
revealing the essence
of the entrepreneur

JOHN A. WOOD

Copyright © 2023 by John A. Wood.

Library of Congress Control Number: 2023911042
ISBN: Hardcover   979-8-3694-9218-5
              Softcover   979-8-3694-9217-8
              eBook   979-8-3694-9216-1

The moral rights of the author have been asserted.

All rights reserved. No part of this book may be reproduced or transmitted in any form or by any means, electronic or mechanical, including photocopying, recording, or by any information storage and retrieval system, without permission in writing from the copyright owner.

All inquiries should be made to the author.

Any people depicted in stock imagery provided by Getty Images are models, and such images are being used for illustrative purposes only.
Certain stock imagery © Getty Images.

Print information available on the last page.

Rev. date: 06/14/2023

To order additional copies of this book, contact:
Xlibris
AU TFN: 1 800 844 927 (Toll Free inside Australia)
AU Local: (02) 8310 8187 (+61 2 8310 8187 from outside Australia)
www.Xlibris.com.au
Orders@Xlibris.com.au
843170

Endorsements for this book

'Who among us has not felt the sense of frustration that comes with knowing that how you live your life doesn't match your philosophy of life? Successful businessman and teacher John Wood has written a wise book that will help you bridge that gap. With John as your guide, you and your organization can go beyond idealism and begin to live from the highest realm of Possibility.'

Barry Brownstein,
Professor Emeritus of Economics and Leadership
University of Baltimore

'Amidst a plethora of self-improvement books, John's writing stands out as a wake-up call, for numerous reasons. For a start, it is challenging, not in a bothersome way, but in a remarkably disarming manner, as it gently directs the reader away from the continuing search for the endless solutions proposed "out there" to problems facing big and small business in particular and, by inference, all of humanity. Instead, it invites the reader to uncover and reflect on two fundamental, innate human faculties, constantly in operation, namely Possibility and Thought – not as interpreted and used conventionally, but understood and seen afresh in ways that are liberating, inspiring and always accessible.

Having known John for decades and been fortunate to have him as a mentor, I have benefited greatly from what he has been pointing to, and have no hesitation in strongly recommending his latest book. It is an invaluable guide that has the potential to last a lifetime.'

Rolf Clausnitzer
Martial-arts teacher
writer and counsellor

'I have seen magic happen when an executive leadership team in business opens to Possibility at an offsite workshop. New unexpected strategic business solutions appear that go beyond linear thinking. Just getting a group of leaders focused on discussing Possibility opens up a new realm, as John explains in this new book. John clearly wants to contribute lasting value for leaders who care about being in service to the common good. This is a must-read for leaders looking to expand the potential of themselves, their teams and business while making a difference in the world.'

Mark Lefko
Workshop Facilitator, Trusted Adviser to Presidents
Board Member and Executive Mentor

'Read this book now ... if you're passionate about being a wildly successful entrepreneur as we enter the uncharted economic and social global territory ahead. This book and the wisdom it shares is based on the radical notion that Possibility – the state of kindness, understanding, wisdom, and common sense – are essential entrepreneurial competencies needed to navigate a new world.'

Craig Neal
Co-Founder – Center for Purposeful Leadership

'*The Business of Possibility* is an immensely powerful and unforgettable book. It will take you on a journey that is simple and yet has profound wisdom on every page. Although focused primarily on business, it will be of equal benefit to readers in their personal lives. In short, this book is life-changing!

It outlines the Fourth Dimension of Business and Organisation, which, while generally not recognised or talked about, lies at the heart of true success. The distinctions between "service" and "being in service" are explored.

Merging "what works" with "what matters" in your organisation creates a culture that sees the team communicating and succeeding at the highest level, but with kindness, understanding, wisdom and common sense.

This doesn't sound like "business talk", does it? And that's our point of difference at Land4Sale and the reason why clients say, "You're a breath of fresh air to work with and you actually give a damn."

I've had the privilege of John Wood's teachings for the past 22 years, which is reflected in how Land4Sale is in business and why we have grown to be the most successful independent organisation in our field. This comes with a willingness to see something new and the intention to be open to Possibility.

The Business of Possibility is a ground-breaking must-read for a start-up business or for an existing business looking for a fresh start.'

Sue Davies
Founder and Managing Director
Land4Sale Western Australia

'I have worked with many, many business owners, and when I reflect on what was their key success factor, it wasn't that they had or employed the best "Skills" – I have seen many highly skilled businesses not reach their potential. It wasn't that they had the best "Systems" – I have seen companies with highly advanced systems fail. And it wasn't **that they had robust** and abundant access to "Finance"… it wasn't any of these factors. All are important. In fact, very important and highly successful businesses were on top of these factors. The standout, however, always comes back to the quality of thinking of the owner and everyone in the organisation … their ability to see Possibility, the "Fourth Dimension" as John calls it … John's insights go to the heart of what matters and, in turn, will lead to what works.'

Mal Di Giulio
Managing Director, Nexia Perth
Chairman, Nexia Australia

'You will be rewarded if you read this book at least twice. The first run through will ignite your curiosity, as this is not your standard business-improvement manual. The second read will give you time to challenge your own beliefs, whether you are an employer or employee of a business or organisation of any size.

John Wood formed and grew a national recreation vehicle business from virtually nothing in the Sixties, and maintained growth despite downturns and recessions and a massive shock to the industry in the late Seventies. Being open to new ideas and constantly fostering the growth of those around him, John pushed the boundaries of traditional business theory, leading to – amongst other things – a new and innovative lifestyle-accommodation concept for the over-55s.

Today, as customers or associates, we come into contact with businesses and organisations that seem to have lost their way and struggle with direction. Quite often this is reflected in the attitude of the people working in customer service. To survive and prosper, a business now needs much more than a healthy cash balance, it needs creative thinking and imagination and to not be wedded to the past. I totally endorse John's latest book as a catalyst for that thinking.'

David Robertson
B ECS Monash
Divisional General Manager (retired), Fleetwood Corporation Ltd

'How can you function well if you do not know how you function? People in positions of authority can facilitate the incredible process of awakening to Possibility most effectively – once they experience it for themselves, they are likely to encourage and support others. This will change the very essence and feel of the organisations they run, through the cumulative effect of more and more employees and contractors understanding themselves, and therefore becoming 100% responsible for themselves and their roles.'

Tony Wilmot, BSc (Chemistry),
retired IT systems analyst/project leader and lawyer

CONTENTS

Foreword xv
Acknowledgments xvii
Possibility In Brief xix
Introduction: why this book xxi

1. My life in Possibility 1
2. What Possibility is and what it isn't 9
   The Trap of our Story 9
   Essential Terms Used In This Book 11
   Distinguishing 'Possibility' from Possibility 13
   Education, Ideologies and Dogmas 13
   The Ambivalence of Memories 14
   True Freedom 18
   I Used To Think I Was Open, And Too Often Still Do ... 22
   Distinguishing Between Openness and Receptivity 23
   Some Popular Mental-Training Models and Possibility ... 26
3. How Possibility can work in any business or organisation ... 29
   How Do We *See* Possibility? 31
   Story: Wifi wonder 32
   Of Two States of Mind – Conscious or Unconscious
      Leadership 33
   Leading By Listening 35
   Entrepreneurial Thinking VS Opportunistic Thinking
      (Conscious VS Unconscious Leadership) 36
   'Team'-Building 42
   The Fourth Element of Business and Organisation: Thought ... 47
   Away With The Fairies, or Swapping Ideas? 47
   An (Old) New Paradigm 48

    Being Half Awake 50
    Element Four: Thought 52
    The Lack Of Consciousness Is All that Ails Capitalism 52
    Story: How Australia won the America's Cup 54
    Our Understanding of Thought Determines our Access
        to Possibility 55
    What Is Missing In Our Understanding? 57
    Story: Allan Helps William *See* 57
    How the Three Other Elements Are Created by Thought 61
    In Summary 63

4. Case study: Implementing Possibility in an organisation 65
    Introduction 66
    Overview 68
    Part One: The Context Necessary for Creating
        Sustainable Community – NLV's Board and Team 68
    Part Two: Creating And Sustaining Harmonious
        Communities Within Each Village so People are
        Encouraged to *See* Possibility 81

5. The Career, Business and Commercial Game 91
    Being In Service Is 'Delivering The Promise' 92
    The Three Faces of Service 94
    Story: The Three Service States of Mind 95
    Key Distinctions Between these Three States of Mind 99
    The Key To Being 'In Service' 101
    Story: It's Only Natural to Have Expectations. But What
        If Your Expectations Have You? 103

6. How to see Possibility using vertical inquiry 107
    Inside-Out Coaching 108
    Delving Into The Unknown, Not Accumulating More
        Information from The Known, Is the Way to Our
        Transformation 108
    Questioning vs Teaching 109
    Inside-Out vs Outside-In 109
    The Vertical Question As A Signpost 111
    The Role of Reflection 113
    Insight: A Moment of Possibility 114

	The Links Joining Vertical Inquiry, Reflection and *Insight*........ 114
	In Summary 115
7.	A checklist for your business or organisation – to show how Possibility can help 116

Finally... 119
Appendix 1: Possibility is not Idealism 121
Appendix 2: The Realm of Possibility Workshop: A (Not-For-Profit) Primer for A Creative Life.. 131

FOREWORD

With this book, John Wood has a clear goal: to be an accelerator for change. For some, this book will be even more than that. It will be your catalyst for a complete transformational experience in your life and your business or organisation.

John Wood is committed to a life-long pursuit of discovery. The quintessential entrepreneur, he has lived an amazing journey of learning and fulfilment. From selling comics as a boy, to creating an ASX-listed company as a young man, John's business experience is comprehensive, authentic and hard-earned.

With remarkable prescience, John foresaw the grey nomad revolution, and was instrumental in establishing the type of modern domestic-tourism industry we see in Australia today. Moreover, as an early champion of the over-55s lifestyle-village concept, he clearly has a keen eye for winning ideas. Big ones at that!

Mirroring the swift trajectory of his company's growth, John just as abruptly retired from business at the tender age of 48. He was seeking something more than the endless pursuit of profit. Luckily for us, he found it, named it and wrote it all down!

John's clarity of vision – based on recurring renewal – is inspirational. Completely free from the shackles of pre-conditioned thinking and programmed beliefs, he helps reveal the enormous scope for personal transformation that dwells, waiting, within us all.

This is crucial because, in transforming yourself, you transform your world – including the business or organisation you seek to influence.

A catalyst for change, John leads us on a powerful journey of discovery. Read on. Learn. Enjoy.

Barry Urquhart
Managing Director, Marketing Focus; Change Management Consultant, Business Strategist, Keynote Speaker; author of *Service Please!, Serves You Right!, Business Imperatives* and *Marketing Magic*; and co-author of *The Jindalee Factor* and *From Black Hole To Blue Sky*-
www.marketingfocus.net.au

ACKNOWLEDGMENTS

With loving gratitude, I acknowledge the people who paid me to work with them, and those who I paid to work with me.

And equally to the many teachers with whom I trained. Notably, I recognise the hundreds of individuals who participated in programs, coaching and training sessions with me. Each of you has been a mirror into my mind. Without knowing, you have facilitated my evolution as a kinder, more understanding human being.

I acknowledge (in alphabetical order) some that left a more profound mark: Ruby Ahern, Michael Bailey, Sydney Banks, David Bodman, Stephanie Chandler, Rolf Clausnitzer, Sue Davies, Alan Farrall, Mal di Giulio, Angus Glendenning, Dean Graham, Robert Kausen, Mark Lefko, Eamonn Leonard, Fred Logue, Andrew MacDonald, Steve de Mol, Craig Neal, John Neil, George Pransky, Linda Pransky, David Robertson, Judy Sedgeman, Frank Trager, Barry Urquhart, Tony Wilmot, Paula Wood, Peter Woods, Brian Zec.

Of course, there are my three primary teachers: mum, May; dad, Jack; and sister, Tanya. Five children: Robert, Lynley, John, Michael and Joanne. Ten grandchildren: Jessica, Georgina, Jackson, Ella, Callan, Dylan, Mathew, Jayden, Saxon and Sienna. And one – to date – great-grandchild: Taneisha. Ronnie, my wife of 44 years, unstinting in supporting, challenging, teaching and loving me for all these years. And my first wife, Christine, and her husband, Michael, with whom we are, importantly, good friends.

My thanks and appreciation to Sean Doyle, editor and Director of Lynk Manuscript Assessment Service, who did his very best to make my writing halfway decent. And to Nanette of Saso Design for the striking cover and elegant interior design of this book.

John Wood

POSSIBILITY IN BRIEF

'For nothing worth proving can be proven,
nor yet disproven …'

ALFRED, LORD TENNYSON

- Possibility exists prior to anything and everything we believe to be 'the truth of the matter'.

- Possibility precedes our conditioned, self-created, rock-solid reality. It is a state of mind beyond what we had believed to be possible, reasonable or, at times, even rational.

- Possibility exists beyond what we currently claim to be irrefutable scientific facts and evidence-based truths.

- Possibility is always available whether we *see* it or not, and it exists (seemingly) independent of us.

- Possibility's profound depth and scope are available to be discovered (and rediscovered) at any time in any place.

- Possibility allows us to *see* new creations and opportunities from the state of awareness that benefits the whole and not just the *seer*.

- Possibility is our original state of awareness when unshackled from our habitual, memory-based, conditioned thinking.

- Possibility is born of fresh Thought (never by recycled thinking, no matter how excellent that thinking may seem) and is a state of intense psychological, philosophical and – although I hesitate to use the word in the context of this book – spiritual freedom.

- Possibility is the realm of creativity, innovation and the solutions to what ails humanity.

INTRODUCTION: WHY THIS BOOK

The quality of our collective thinking alone determines the success, mediocrity or failure of our business or organisation and, more critically, whether they serve the common good.

Entrepreneurship has been an important thread throughout my life. In this book I will demonstrate how *seeing* Possibility has contributed to success in both my business and personal life. I'll include some key points along the way – some of the many times I failed to *see* Possibility and, in my earlier years, when I was *seeing* it but didn't realise what was occurring in my mind.

I will also demonstrate how working from Possibility – the state of kindness, understanding, wisdom and common sense – is *the unrecognised yet most critically important element* in all businesses, not-for-profits and government organisations.

Since the age of six, my life has revolved around businesses and organisations, with considerable contact with governments. That world demanded I evolve in understanding myself and others. I escaped from school at 15 and, with my first pay packet as an 'office boy', purchased two books. One was Dale Carnegie's *How to Win Friends and Influence People*, a wonderfully wise, insightful contribution to the common good. The second was a book on Plato. I can't remember its title, couldn't understand it and never got past p. 3. These two purchases were indicative of the direction in which I was looking – and have continued to look ever since.

In 1990, I retired from the business I started in 1964, aged 22 (on the driveway of my parent's home). I discovered that what I *saw*, from a young age, seemed to be missing from the understanding of many of those representing Western capitalism: the people in businesses, NGOs, governments and their agencies.

Exploring, discovering and sharing what I've found and, more recently, writing about what I *see* missing in organisations, is my work – my purpose. This slim book outlines the paradigm shift desperately needed to transform 'the organisation', of any and all descriptions – from businesses to governments – into instruments that deliver the promise implicit in their very existence: that is, being genuinely in service to the common good.

Make no mistake, I am an advocate for a free-enterprise system. But I propose a system very different to the one that has evolved, that purports to be but so often is not in service to the common good. It is, rather, in service to the egos and bank balances of those in leadership positions. In terms of delivering this promise to the common good, corporations, governments and other organisations are performing average at best, badly to shoddily at worst.

This guide points to the way forward. It doesn't say what we should do with our institutions – businesses great and small, our NGOs, our different levels of government. It says they are all a product of YOU and ME, we who lead and work in them. It explains how we are the transforming agents, how it's we who need to transform ourselves – and, in so doing, transform our organisations.

If you don't already understand that the problem is you and me, you will, I hope, come to understand that the future of your world and, consequently, the entire world rests squarely on your shoulders. The buck stops with you and me. You could say that when we don't understand our individual, pivotal roles, then we the people simply 'fiddle while Rome burns'.

We – you and I – are the starting point, the way forward, the transforming element and therefore the solution to what each of us wants in our heart of hearts *and* in the organisations that serve us and that we work in, depend on and/or own.

This book explains how excellence, mediocrity and shoddiness are created moment by moment within our multi-faceted world of organisations. It speaks to how sustainability is created or destroyed. It is the book of the genuine entrepreneurial spirit.

CHAPTER 1

MY LIFE IN POSSIBILITY

*Possibility is a state of awareness in which we
see new beginnings.*

What follows are some of the ideas that, through my life, have manifested in my mind – within The Realm of Possibility – and the opportunities that were revealed to me and which I acted upon. Most of them are quite run of the mill; some are more ambitious.

Each one of us has these and other types of *insights*. Mostly, we don't recognise their potential or understand where they come from. Many of us don't act on them – impossibility gets in our way.

As you read snippets from my life, you may notice ways that Possibility is showing up in your life.

You will read that Possibility materialised for me primarily in business, though not only there. And it showed up early! Your *insights* might show up in some other field and at any time.

Some of the limitless facets of Possibility are: *seeing* opportunity where others don't, and *seeing* the scope for innovation where none was previously *seen*. Another is in recognising the challenges likely to be thrown up and the ways to overcome them. Yet another, and probably the most important, is in experiencing our innate courage and determination to execute the idea/s *seen* within The Realm of Possibility.

1946: My first entrepreneurial idea was as a five-year-old. I collected and sold nasturtium flowers in used food jars for a half-penny or penny a jar, depending on the jar size. They were bought by residents and passers-by of the block of flats in which Mum, Dad and I lived. We came from 'the wrong side of the tracks' and the flowers came for free from a nearby demolition site. That was the (early start) of my business career.

1952: Aged 11, during the Christmas holidays, I set up a comics exchange in a corner of my parents' shop. I had collected comics since I learnt to read and kept them in pristine condition – a useful aspect of my obsessive tendency.

The business idea was 'one of mine for one of yours plus a penny'. And for those that didn't have a penny, 'one of mine for two of yours'. I earned over £12 and, as some of you might know, there were 144 pennies to a pound. I also massively increased the 200 or so comics I started out with. Business was brisk during those six weeks and it wasn't just kids who wanted to trade. People of all ages did!

1958: In my first job as an office boy, aged 16, with The Royal Exchange Assurance (a British fire, accident and marine insurance company), I purchased salvaged goods destined for auction, and I sold them to family, friends and neighbours. The company recovered more for their salvage than from sending it to auction, and I made extra income. This was the first time, I was told (probably falsely), that an employee had *seen* to do this since 1720, when the company was founded. It sounded impressive at the time; seems more like BS today.

Apart from changing the manager's blotting paper, date stamp, filling his fountain pen with ink, and going out each day to buy his lunch, I had other jobs such as filing letters, insurance proposals and copies of expiry and renewal notices. My predecessor hadn't done a good job of filing (it cost him his job) and, seeing as I was an organised individual, I put it all in pristine order.

However, a long-unaddressed aspect of the filing that had existed well prior to the person I replaced, and had worsened during his tenure, was a back room where the floor was knee-deep in unfiled material. It was very dated, some of it going back decades (written in copperplate handwriting).

With much of it scattered, in busted binders and broken files, and with no semblance of a system for finding anything, it was a bureaucrat's nightmare. On the few occasions I was asked to search for something, I came up empty-handed. And I was a beaver. It was beyond rare that anyone rummaging through that pile found the document they sought.

I had what I thought was a bright idea. I *saw* the obvious – the time-wasting, frustration and hopelessness of the situation for those trying to find any documents in that mess – and decided to fix it. Without asking anyone, I obtained 16 very large chaff bags. Armed with them and a getaway truck I'd lined up, I went into the office early on a Sunday. Sorting out what little could be salvaged, I put that neatly aside then filled the chaff bags with the rest and took them to the tip.

Now, in the late 1950s, children were to be seen and not heard. In the same way, an office boy had no authority and received little respect. You were just expected to jump to it when asked.

On the Monday morning, Alan Blunt, a senior underwriter, went to look for a document in that room. I couldn't believe it! When he opened the door, he was greeted by organisation – a neat row of the remaining material – but not what he was looking for. He immediately came looking for me. On being told what I had done, he headed for the assistant manager's door. Quickly returning, he told me to see the boss.

Angus Glendenning was my first boss and a great bloke. In response to his question as to why I had done what I had done, I told him something like this: 'Sir, it seemed to me that it was a problem that could not be sorted out. Most, if not all the files were broken, and their contents scattered. Those still intact that contained relevant files, I kept and put in order. Finding a document was near impossible. The job of trying to sort the mess would take days and, as most of the stuff was redundant, it would be a waste of resources. It was clear to me that if I simply got rid of the ongoing pain, within a short time everyone would see the benefit of being rid of it.'

His response was short and something like: 'John, I'm glad you took the initiative. Next time please ask me.'

1960: At 19 years of age, with hard-earned savings from a thrifty approach and a financial and mentoring partnership with my father, I took on a dirt-cheap, badly run-down delicatessen in Perth's poorest neighbourhood. Its five prior owners had all gone broke.

We approached our bank, but they wanted nothing to do with our venture and strongly cautioned us against going ahead. Although wafer-thin on finance, we proceeded anyway, based on a very simple but out-of-the-box idea detailed below.

Within 12 months we increased turnover 600 percent. According to the sales and deliverymen from our various suppliers, it had become the best-performing deli in the Perth metropolitan area.

The neighbourhood was very poor, made up of pensioners, single parents, disabled people and families on welfare. Only a small percentage of the people who lived there were employed. 'Maniana' was a State Housing Area. In later years it was demolished and replaced.

Aside from the excellent shopkeeping employed, such as an increased range of the best produce, great presentation and delivering the promise to our customers (see Chapter 5, 'Being in service is delivering the promise', our key finance strategy (original idea) was the simple but crucial difference between success and failure.

We discovered during our inquiries that each of our predecessors had extended credit to their customers, and that made up around 85 percent of their sales. With that demographic, the resultant level of bad debt had overwhelmed every previous shopkeeper and had been the primary, if not the only, reason for their failure. As you read on, you'll come to *see* why it was a symptom, not a cause.

What amazed us was that, although crystal clear to anyone that could actually *see what is,* each owner had continued to offer credit, believing (I can only guess) that they couldn't do business without offering it. (Giving credit was general practice in small businesses back then.)

We decided on a zero-credit policy.

Initially, because of how attractive the shop had become, those in the area who paid cash and had previously shopped elsewhere started to shop with us. Those that wanted credit, which was the majority of the customers we started out with, went where they could get it. If they couldn't go elsewhere because they had previously blotted their copybook, they paid cash with us.

Eventually, the individuals with poor payment habits ran out of easily accessible shops from which they could get credit. With no options left, they returned to shop with us, but this time paying cash – a benefit to them and a decision that kept us in business.

Our 'fresh idea' was that while it would take some time (actually only a few months), we were certain that we would regain and keep their business (and our solvency) by not giving them credit. Taking this step was easier said than done. I stuck to my guns in the face of pleading from some and abuse from others. And it worked. At our deli, the customers had no option but to budget their weekly outgoings and purchase only their necessities. It was a simple idea, but one necessary (in that area) to having a sustainable business. It was, for the first time in its short history, really in service to the common good.

1963: By 21, I was working seven days a week, including Christmas Days and Good Fridays, from 7 am to 7 pm, or in the summer months as late as there were customers to serve. As you can imagine, this lifestyle was restrictive – I wanted to move on. We sold the business at a good profit.

I placed an advertisement in the classifieds of our main daily. Having listed my abilities and experience, I was invited to apply for several positions, and accepted one in which I had zero experience. The company, Modern Caravans, primarily a hirer but also a manufacturer and seller of caravans, had not sold a single unit in the four months prior to my starting. Though I had not holidayed in one, not even looked inside one, I sold 44 caravans in five months. Experience is over-rated when it comes to succeeding. As you read through this guide, you will see why other attributes – primarily our state of awareness in *seeing* Possibility, and an understanding of how and why we humans think, feel and act in the ways we do – are so much more important.

1964: *Seeing* that the company was straightjacketed by its rigid thinking, I resigned one Friday night and started my own business the next morning from the driveway of my parents' home. It was 24 February 1964.

At 22, with the briefest experience under my belt and (pre-Australia's currency conversion in 1966) with £1000 (part of my savings from the deli), I started Fleetwood Caravans in partnership with my father (he also put in £1000). Buying a very old second-hand caravan for £100, we renovated it and sold it for £225. I worked out that we earned about 2/6 (two shillings and six pence) per hour each for our labour. But it was a satisfying start.

I clearly recall in that first week, as we worked on renovating that old caravan, saying to Dad that within ten years this business would be the largest company of its type in Australia. Dad may well have put my thoughts down to youthful audacity, yet I *saw* Possibility as clearly as I had with how to transform the derelict deli three years earlier. Ten years on, Fleetwood had become just that.

1964–1990: During this period, Fleetwood was a very creative and innovative organisation. Moving within a few months from my parents' driveway in suburban Perth, it expanded rapidly through vertical and horizontal integration. We were instrumental in transforming the marketing, selling, servicing, insuring and the repair of all types of recreational vehicles (RVs), as well as the importation and distribution of camping gear, RV parts and accessories. Fleetwood developed and refurbished caravan parks, pioneered park homes, and designed and built the first village to accommodate them.

By 1972, we had created, with the blessing of the Tourism Commission of Western Australia, the 'Sir David Brand Awards' for tourism. These were later expanded upon and replicated by the other States, culminating in Australia's National Tourism Awards. These awards are acclaimed and still celebrated annually.

Our vision and detailed plans for re-creating aspects of the industry were also embraced by the state and local governments, and proved transformative. The industry and, more importantly, the community are still experiencing the benefits of that work today in the form of a popular model of Lifestyle Villages for the over-45s.

In 1990, aged 48, I resigned as CEO and Chairman of Fleetwood, by then a publicly listed company on the Australian Stock Exchange. We had navigated many very difficult economic periods. I was ready for a fresh start. Disposing of my shareholdings in a way that secured capital and fresh input for the company's future, I resigned from all external board positions and made a complete break with business. I had *seen* Possibility in other areas of my life, and I would now follow that vision.

1993: At 51, somewhat grounded by personal *insights*, and as a consequence of meetings with Sydney Banks (a Scottish welder whose epiphany has transformed the life of thousands – Google him) and limited training with a number of leading coaches in the field, I opened the doors to a centre in Perth to share this understanding. The Philosophy of Everyday Living Centre was the first in its field outside North America. Although I lacked formal qualifications in psychology, philosophy or spirituality, the Centre was highly successful, as evaluated by the results of the services it offered to people and organisations.

During the life of the Centre, apart from hundreds of programs and countless coaching and counselling sessions, we developed a hard-copy magazine and later a digital version, and every two months distributed 22,000 copies globally to foster the work of Sydney Banks and others in the field. We opened a small office in Bend, Oregon, US, and developed a comprehensive website taking the work of the practitioners and authors to the world for the first time. During its relatively short life, we attracted students from all over Australia, New Zealand, Asia, Europe, the UK and the US. We delivered programs and worked with organisations internationally, including some as large as the British Broadcasting Commission. It was an amazing journey of discovery.

2006: I retired from the Centre. Although the results being achieved were good and the Centre was continuing to grow and evolve, I didn't feel happy with my leadership; nor was I satisfied with either my own level of understanding or that of my colleagues – and there was no one, I thought, who could step up and deliver the promise in the way I saw was needed. Each of us was doing the best we could see or *see* to do and, with my obsession for 'delivering the promise', I was not satisfied we were doing that.

Weeks later I was diagnosed with prostate cancer. Thus began a journey in supporting my body's healing. I embraced a transformed lifestyle, which continues to this day.

2010: A seminal experience for me. During a retreat in Peru, I *saw* more deeply into the Realm of original Thought and Possibility with a level of clarity not previously *seen*. My previous book, *Possibility ... a State of Mind*, as well as The Realm of Possibility Project and Workshop (outlined in Appendix 2), were born from this experience.

2012: Although my condition stabilised – probably as a result of my dramatically changed lifestyle, several conventional health-retreat experiences, and other alternative experimentations since first diagnosed – the cancer started to grow and move. I decided to have my prostate surgically removed: the common-sense step to take. (Regular tests show that I remain in the clear.)

2013: At bedtime on 27 December, I read an essay on anthropogenic global warming. I had been concerned about, and for some years (with my wife) involved in the philosophy and practice of sustainability. One of the dozens of articles, essays and several books I had read, this article cut deep.

I was unable to sleep, tossing and turning in mental anguish. It seemed clear that unless humanity dramatically reduced and ultimately eliminated its dependence on fossil fuels, the planet would likely become too hot to support life as we know it. I felt the drive to dedicate my experience and energy towards redressing global warming.

Although it was abundantly clear that the number-one challenge facing humanity was the omnipresence of impossibility thinking (a state of mind I will flesh out later), the escalating emissions of greenhouse gases from fossil fuel and the refusal to redress these issues were impossibility thinking in action, and clearly the number-two challenge (albeit a symptom of the first).

At 3 am I started writing an action plan for Climate Action Now (CAN), which was to be an organisation dedicated to educating and motivating people globally to dramatically reduce and, where possible, eliminate their CO_2 emissions. I was 72, and Possibility was still manifesting in action.

2014: Again I *saw* that, within The Realm of Possibility, we can change direction on a dime when we *see* the obvious. On 4 November, in a Skype conversation with a friend, colleague and climate-change activist in Canada, I realised that the rationale for starting CAN was no longer valid for me. Global circumstances had changed dramatically. Climate scientists were now being taken seriously by more and more people worldwide, especially by governments and their policy makers. The job CAN was designed to do now appeared redundant. Larger, more powerful organisations were better equipped. It was time to move on.

2019: *Possibility ... a State of Mind* was published, the first Realm of Possibility Workshop was facilitated, and the initial Realm of Possibility Development Group commenced. Possibility awaits you and me! What form will it take?

2020: This book is published. Specifically addressing the world of business and organisations of all types, it is a companion piece to *Possibility ... a State of Mind*. What impact might it have? The answer is in our minds and hearts – in The Realm of Possibility ...

CHAPTER 2

WHAT POSSIBILITY IS AND WHAT IT ISN'T

'It is pure illusion to think that an opinion that passes down from century to century, from generation to generation, may not be entirely false.'

PIERRE BAYLE

Story, fable, myth and metaphor can be created to encourage kindness, understanding, wisdom and common sense. Stories are also used to elicit fear, hatred and extremism, or simply to entertain or educate. But no story can get to the essence of who we or others are. It's this essence, this core aspect of you and me that is beyond any story, especially our personal story we repeatedly tell ourselves.

So why do we use stories? We use them to educate, entertain, engage and enrol our fellow humans. But if taken as 'the truth', they are a trap.

THE TRAP OF OUR STORY

My story, your story, our collective stories and their collective stories – any story ever told or yet to be told – is the trap most of us are entangled in today or will get lost in tomorrow.

A story can be a catalyst for healing, or it can keep us stuck in anxiety, worry and upset. Useful stories can be signposts, pointing towards a deeper reality within the teller and listener. Unhelpful stories come from and feed upon fears and myths existing within our memories. These are our personal, family and cultural stories. Innocently we reinforce our worldviews by eating up stories that feed them: stories about our view of our self and others, our fantasies, fears and imaginings. Seeking the security of the known, we dig ourselves deeper into our ever-enlarging story, creating and embellishing 'the truth of it' as we go.

We call our stories by many different names: reality, my life, how I am, the way I was born and raised, my conditioning, my gender, my race, nationality, religion, politics, identity. We see them all as 'the truth' of who we are – and, just as regrettably, who others are.

But listen – we are not our story! We never have been. We're neither our past nor our present story, nor any future elaboration we think into being and believe to be the substance of our life ... as being who we are. Stories are an illusory construct we think into existence, appearing in our mind as 'reality'. And they are the only reality we know – until we make up or *see* another. Our imagined story – no matter what it is – is the counterfeit reality we imprison our self in. And so it remains until we wake up from that dream and actually *see what is*, not what we remember it to be.

Who we are capable of being exists beyond these stories and is hidden from us, veiled by the story we create about ourselves, about others and every aspect of life. Our stories are created anytime from a nanosecond ago right back to our beginning, maybe even before that. They manifest as ideas, experiences, beliefs, opinions, judgements, philosophies, values and knowledge around all that we consider good or evil, right or wrong, fact or fiction.

They all include what we think works best and what we think matters most. We accept from others or create afresh in our mind these stories, in which we innocently ensnare ourselves – surrendering our freedom from *seeing what is*; preferring to live in the pleasure and pain of our make-believe world. In that process, we become 'our story'. Being buried in it, we imagine ourselves to be the empowered creation or disempowered victim of our past, or current or future life and circumstances. This we claim as 'reality'.

In awakening to and *seeing* the trap of our never-ending stories, we are freed to experience Possibility – The Realm that exists beyond all stories, but which we may also, quite innocently, turn into our new 'I have found the truth' story. Possibility is *seen* (only ever *seen*) in the moment we *see* beyond our story. In that awakening, we *see* and understand how we have trapped ourselves in an endless story. It is then we start to gain clarity in regard to 'Life and The Game of Living'.

In glimpsing the reality that precedes the formation of our stories, we can recognise that *absolutely everything* emanates from what I call Possibility. But remember, as you read on, there are no answers to be found in any story, however factually true or painfully tragic (including this story). Instead, look for 'reality' within your quietened mind and softened heart. Those are the gateways to awakening. The answers we seek await us in The Realm of Possibility.

ESSENTIAL TERMS USED IN THIS BOOK

Throughout this book, key words and phrases are used to convey meanings often different from their general use and meaning.

Thought (with a capital 'T') is used to signify the Life energy enabling and creating the reality we call our life. Within the context of this book, 'Thought' in its unformed (energetic) state is The Realm of Possibility. I do not claim to understand what Thought is specifically – this book is my attempt to flesh out the concept of Thought within the context of my own experiences.

thinking (with a small 't') is the form this Thought energy takes within our mind as our moment-to-moment cognition (thinking) and is the way we see or *see* and therefore experience our personal reality.

Possibility (with a capital 'P') is where the abstract, unfathomable domain of Thought meets our personal reality in the form of original ideas, brand-new concepts, fresh starts and transformed relationships. In a state of Possibility, we *see* new discoveries, previously un*seen* inventions, innovations and opportunities. More importantly, and fundamental to the lifeblood of this book, it is The Realm of our transformation from who we mistakenly think we are to who, in our essence, we really are. It is The Realm in which each of us can experience a profound feeling of kindness, deep understanding, great wisdom and *insightful* common sense – the mantra throughout this text. When directly experiencing life from that state of Possibility, irrespective of our circumstances, we are at our most empowered. And in that state we take whatever next step it is we *see* to take in achieving our goal.

awareness (with a small 'a') along with aware, awake, conscious, consciousness and understanding (used interchangeably) signifies that we have actually *seen* our thinking as the source of our reality and understand what state we are experiencing in each moment. Our clarity of awareness is the degree to which we are awake in the moment to our thinking and the feelings generated by that thinking via our five senses – conscious of our beliefs, opinions and judgements; aware of our story around our life and

Life as a mystery. It is the extent to which we *see* our thinking and feelings for being just that, not 'the truth.'

Life (with a capital 'L') is my best stab at the mysterious source of life-giving Thought. Life is called by many other names: God, Universal Mind, Universal Intelligence, and more. I am agnostic. I hasten to add that from personal *insights*, there seems to be an unfathomable essence to you and me (and maybe all else) that exists *a priori* to anything I or you make up about it, which fuels all aspects of my and your life, and possibly the totality of life as you and I know it. I call that mysterious source (if there is one) Life. When experiencing life from a state of Possibility, I feel closest to what I sense as being the fountain … that which I call Life.

see **(italicised)** along with *seer, seeing, seen, saw* and *insight* denote a deepened awareness into, a profound clarity around, and at its peak, revelation emanating from fresh Thought within The Realm of Possibility.

what is **(italicised)** is *seeing* through (unchained from) our imaginings, already formed ideas, conditioned beliefs, opinions, judgements and knowledge (all our lifelong accumulated stories) to *seeing* the actuality of *what is* presenting before us. This is the only true freedom.

kindness, understanding, wisdom and common sense denote a state of intense goodwill, sensitivity, deep perception and respect for all others and for the natural world.

the common good: Can anyone, in all honesty, foresee the consequences, intended or otherwise, of one's actions – whether they will work for or against the common good, or whether they will matter one way or the other? When used, this term refers to actions that will, on balance, do no harm. They will be actions that foster environmental, social, economic and societal sustainability. Above all else, they will be actions taken neither from an ideological, religious or socio-political stance, but from a state of kindness, understanding, wisdom and common sense, and will unite '*what really works*' and '*what really matters*'.

our story refers to the self-created accumulation of illusions we live in: our unrecognised prison.

what really works and what really matters **(italicised)**: see 'Possibility' above.

DISTINGUISHING 'POSSIBILITY' FROM POSSIBILITY

'If something can realistically happen, it's a possibility.' That dictionary definition is all well and good, but it's not the meaning referred to in this guide. Beyond this limited definition is a state of awareness in which our transformation can occur and seemingly unlimited Possibility is *seen*. Within this realm, Possibility can be an enthralling reality and a life-altering state, holding the potential to transform our life and consequently our world ... and our influence on it.

Explorers of Life, venturing into The Realm of where we create reality, have directly and deeply experienced fresh Thought – the genesis of Possibility. They've discovered the unconditional kindness, understanding, wisdom and common sense that exist before the values, culture and conditioning that we inherit and expand upon, and that incarcerate us. It is in that realm that we, too, *see* and experience Possibility and our own transformation. Possibility is the state in which we *see what is* and create a new future.

Without *seeing* into The Realm of Possibility, we repeat (to a lesser or greater degree) our 'Groundhog Day' experience of life. On experiencing fresh Thought, we *see* Possibility. Our vision is attuned to *seeing* and creating a new future. *Seeing* Possibility and creating our life afresh might just be our most useful daily yoga – re-creating our relationships, organisations, and the world.

EDUCATION, IDEOLOGIES AND DOGMAS

The transformation many seek, and that which humanity desperately needs, cannot take place amid the mental maze and limitations of our existing education, ideologies and dogmas. Aware of it or not, each of us lives each moment either *seeing* Possibility (and living from a state of kindness, understanding, wisdom and common sense) or failing to *see* it – blinded to Possibility by our story called, 'I know the truth'.

It is through those who live regularly influenced by Possibility that the world transforms person by person. Once you *see* Possibility, you will hear their voices, recognise their perspectives, and be touched by their kind and fearless hearts. With these kindred spirits you can create a new world – a world increasingly under the influence of kindness, understanding, wisdom and common sense, a world where more are *seeing* Possibility rather than impossibility.

In short, Possibility presents us with the opportunity to transform ourselves and the world we think we know. Imagine what the world would look like if Possibility was being experienced in the minds and hearts of all humanity – or even in ten percent of us. What would your world look like? What would your relationships look like? What would your work look like?

And how do we allow Possibility to come alive in our life and therefore in our organisations?

THE AMBIVALENCE OF MEMORIES

The repository of all fear is memory.

For simplicity, imagine memories falling into two groups: memories having *practical use* in our lives and memories having *no practical use*.

Each group has two sub-groups: non-fearful memories, and fearful memories.

Memories Having Practical Use (useful/less emotionally charged memories)		Memories Having Little Or No Practical Use (more emotionally charged memories)	
Non-fearful examples	Fearful examples	Non-fearful examples	Fearful examples
Reading, tying shoelaces, washing dishes, speaking, driving a car, cooking, brushing teeth.	Avoiding accidents, walking around a snake, looking both ways before crossing a road, being careful when handling poison, saving for a rainy day, understanding high-voltage electricity.	Fond memories of a childhood romance, recalling a beautiful sunset, the feeling of joy when thinking of a loved one, remembering a past glorious moment.	Animosity towards authority, phobia of flying, anxiety with public speaking, racial hatred, procrastination.

Memories having *practical use* are mostly a blessing ('mostly' will become clearer). Without these memories we could not repeat yesterday's most basic tasks, both non-fearful and fearful.

Memories having *little or no practical use*, even non-fearful examples, if not awake to them, keep us from being present to *what is* and to Possibility.

Much more debilitating are fearful examples of memories that have *little or no practical use*. If these are not *seen* and therefore understood, they will invariably blight our life.

The following can be said to be true of all memory, whether *practical* or of *little or no practical use*:

- What we experience day-to-day – our ideas, beliefs, opinions, judgements and knowledge – is, overwhelmingly, delivered for use directly from our memory.

- Irrespective of its content or detail, memory delivers our moment-to-moment experience of living – whether experienced as good, bad or indifferent.

- All memories, whether we deem them positive or negative, useful or otherwise, are imaginings re-created from our past posing as our moment-to-moment personal reality – as 'our personal truth'.

That is why memory is both a blessing and a curse: a blessing in that we can consciously re-create what we experienced in our yesterdays, and a curse in that we, in the main, unconsciously re-create what we experienced in those yesterdays. And that is what has us living primarily in impossibility thinking.

As a result of not understanding this, we are blindly indiscriminate in what we re-create in each moving moment and have no idea we are doing so – the crux of the human dilemma! Our 'Groundhog Day' lives on day after day. Memories of all descriptions – not 'stone walls' or 'iron bars' – create the prison in which we live limited and limiting lives.

It is our lack of understanding of and misuse of memory that has the world stuck in the eternal mire of conflict, strife and unsustainability.

It is the memory of yesterday's grievances in which relationships are trapped that prevents a fresh start.

It is memory that maintains the *status quo*.

An example: while on one hand it is enabling to have a certain skill (another name for applied memory), such as farming the land in a particular way, on the other hand that very knowledge (another name for memory) can get in the way of discovering how to farm in a way that would be more environmentally sustainable or economically viable.

Knowing how to farm is memory having *practical use*, so you could call it a blessing. But is it a blessing or a curse when a well-intentioned but misguided farmer persists in working the land in a way that progressively turns arable soil into salty wasteland? It has become a memory having *little or no practical use*.

When we add a fearful memory into that farmer's psychological mix, such as being punished severely as a small boy for experimenting with new ideas, he may be rendered impotent – unable to respond to the critical need for discovering how to prevent further loss of his farmland to salt and how to reclaim the land already degraded.

A long-forgotten decision to tread only the path of tradition, in this case the family farming tradition, has become his prison.

Our farmer's unrecognised fear of trying something new might be strong enough to ensure the extinction of good farming land and the destruction of a 100-year-old family business.

Memory has its practical uses. It has its fond memories. It is also home to all fear and fear's offspring – arrogance, ignorance, authority, power and control.

Is it not our individual and collective fearful past memories that block our psychological freedom and the flowering of love, understanding, wisdom and common sense, and the noble feelings that epitomise the deeper core nature of humankind?

And therefore, is it not our core nature that will bring into being:

- love and understanding within family;
- wisdom and common sense on earth;
- sustainability of the earth in agriculture, mining, industry and commerce;
- food, shelter, education and equality of opportunity for all;
- the transformation of government and business into servants of the people?

I am suggesting that kindness, understanding, wisdom and common sense are expressions of psychological freedom, our inherent nature manifesting naturally – not something we learn; not something contained in commandments, chiselled on stone tablets, handed down, that we must follow for fear of punishment or to seek favour in the hereafter.

Fear we learn. Fear is part and parcel of memory. Peace, love and other freedoms like wisdom, common sense, gratitude and joy come from a deeper place within – a place from before the formation of memory. Before memory – that is, before we think – lies the realm of original Thought, and within that realm exists Possibility.

Thought, inarguably, is the source of all human experience. Thought is not to be confused with the brain – the physical organ that enables the human manifestation of Thought and our sensory experience. As the origin of human 'beingness', Thought is the natural order of things. The rest we make up as we go along, unconsciously utilising this gift of Thought with which to create, live, think, see or *see*, feel, taste, touch and smell.

Thinking, i.e. all mental activity, is the form that Thought takes within our mind. Thought is the mysterious element that provides humanity with the capacity to think, to create our moment-to-moment reality of living, and the free will to experience and navigate our way through life.

It is to the degree that we are conscious of Thought (i.e. understand; are aware of; are awake to) that we:

- *see* that we think;
- *see* what we are thinking;
- *see* that it is in thinking, whatever it is we are thinking, that we are creating and experiencing our moment-to-moment reality as human beings;
- *see* in each unfolding moment that we are experiencing our life from Possibility or impossibility;
- *see* that from the realm of Possibility, fear is our servant;
- *see* that from blind fear (a state of impossibility), fear is our master.

So, if you can *see* this, you will realise that all memories, of *practical* or of *little or no practical use*, fearful or otherwise, are re-created in the moment via our thinking, and do not represent 'the truth'. And in *seeing* this, we will experience psychological freedom – freedom from our past.

Freedom from the memories dominating your life does not mean you will not experience fear. That, as pointed out earlier, would not serve you well. But it does mean you will no longer be fearful of fear itself, nor blinded by it. Fear will be experienced and understood for what it is: memory carried from the past into the moment and projected into the future to either take care of you and your loved ones, or to disable and render you impotent.

We might call fear an illusion, an illusion that might be helpful or one that might be a 'ball and chain' anchoring you to a painful place in time that no longer exists.

Practical fear keeps you from burning yourself with fire, while unrecognised fear can keep you from using fire at all. Practical fear is coupled with wisdom and common sense, and can help. Misunderstood fear can be immobilising and self-destructive when you re-create a past traumatic event, an event that is not happening now and is unlikely to ever happen again but still gets in the way and prevents you, for example, from having a loving sexual relationship with a partner.

See your past (just another name for memory) for what it is – something that no longer exists, carried through time via memory, re-created in the moment and projected into the future – and be free.

TRUE FREEDOM

When frozen by fear, we see only impossibility.

Released from the straightjacket of our accumulated ideas, beliefs, opinions and judgements, and freed from the grip of our memories, positive or negative (about ourselves, others and life in general), we experience true freedom.

Such freedom cannot be understood without also understanding fear, its source and its impact. Fear comes from our capacity to think and is a re-creation of aspects of our past. Fear blights the lives of individuals, is the bane of humanity and the antithesis of freedom. Fear epitomises the problematic aspect of having memory.

PSYCHOLOGICAL FREEDOM IS THE ONLY TRUE FREEDOM

In not understanding memory and our emotionally charged, fearful thinking around aspects of our past, we live under the tyranny of yesterday.

At its best, memory can still be an unwelcome intrusion into our moment-to-moment experience of life. Memory distorts the simple reality of *what is*.

Looking at two roses, we may think we prefer a yellow to a red one. We may think this one is small in relation to the one we just looked at and which we liked more. Lost in our memory, we miss *seeing* the beauty and wonder of nature before us. We may even think, 'I don't like roses, their thorns ruin their appeal'.

Our memory-based checklist of what we like and don't like gets in our way. On and on, we compare and contrast the flowers' beauty, splendour and prettiness, and so miss *seeing* and appreciating *what is*.

At worst, our memory (including all irrational fears) renders us frozen in time and lost in our past. Walking down the road, I turn a corner. A dog, off its lead, bounds towards me. Panicked, I turn and start running, screaming, 'Call your dog, call your dog!'

Behind me, I hear the owner whistle and sense the dog is returning to him.

I look back. Yes. Relief! Heart racing, cold sweat on my face, I gasp for air as I hesitantly turn. I start walking back towards the owner. He apologises and assures me his dog is friendly, gentle and would not bite anyone. He explains that the dog was running after me as he does when playing a game with his children. It's a dog's natural instinct. But I'm not reassured. I have a fear of dogs.

Of course, to live life unfettered by memory is impossible, as it is to live a life free of fear. Nor is it necessary, or even desirable.

However, psychological freedom is possible and desirable, and it 'comes with the territory' when we live life with the awareness of Possibility and its deeper reality of kindness, understanding, wisdom and common sense. Psychological freedom is necessary if we are to experience the manifestation of our core nature, rather than living blighted by the blindness of our dead yesterdays that, at their worst, manifest today as extreme fear, hatred, jealousy, envy and greed.

The antidote to the paralysis of fearful thinking lies in understanding more fully its root cause: the problematic aspects of our memory. Through understanding the nature of memory, we can experience life freed from the crippling effects of frightening or traumatic past events. With this understanding comes a life of psychological freedom.

OUR MEMORY HAS US FALSELY BELIEVING WE 'KNOW'

Our inbuilt susceptibility to becoming constricted and controlled by the mental boundaries of memory (our conditioned thinking) started when we were born, maybe earlier. As we grew, each new experience both influenced and was skewed by our developing worldview. All we saw, heard, felt, smelt, tasted and thought about was added to our internal narrative ... the story we became wedded to and identified with. As each experience was collated and filed in our mind's storage system, we became more and more lost in the thicket of those memories. We became more and more convinced that we knew 'the truth' of who we and they are.

We call these accumulated experiences by many names: upbringing, conditioning, learning, scripting, study, education, training, habituation, acclimatisation, inculcation, culturalisation and familiarisation. We call it 'life experience', 'national identity', even 'self-realisation' and 'revelation' – and much more.

Everything, even our most profound *insights*, is potential input to our growing blindness. The inherent trap in our accumulation of knowledge and information, even our past insights and most powerful epiphanies, is that we innocently come to believe we actually know 'the truth' of something – of anything! Our conviction in our beliefs, opinions, judgements, lifelong experiences and, dare I say it again, in our most profound of revelations, or in our blind belief in the miracles of others' revelations, makes it so. We are not conscious that our view of the world is formed and is being re-formed and reinforced by looking through the preconceived notions of our past. Layer upon layer …

We are asleep to how our newest discovery, rather than facilitating us to *see what is,* becomes our newest 'truth'. And that is because we don't understand what is required to open again, again, and yet again to Possibility … further opening to our innate faculty of awareness. Even having experienced an awakening to Possibility, it is blindingly easy to become lost in that memory. It's so easy to slip from that level of awareness and to once more see life through that once-original thinking, believing 'This time I have found "the truth".' But that is now the past and, if unrecognised for what it is, a state of impossibility.

Our challenge is to be able to live in the peaceful and sustainable way felt so profoundly in that moment of awakening, and to continue in an ever-growing state of kindness, understanding, wisdom and common sense. And make no mistake, this is the case even when our conviction that we know 'the truth' is based on:

- a high IQ;
- an advanced education;
- decades of investigation and research;
- deep meditative practice;
- having experienced that beautiful feeling (from entering The Realm of Possibility) and being told at that time that it was due to a direct connection with God, Allah, Universal Mind or our particular Saint or Sage.

When our convictions are supported and reinforced by a close association with like-minded people, it can be doubly difficult to *see* because we innately desire to stay connected with others and belong to 'the group'. This is how cults are formed.

Even when a guru we love and respect has been profoundly influenced by *seeing* Possibility and tells us 'this is the truth', it's easy to believe them and in doing so become lost in that belief. We make excuses for them, thinking they are immune to 'smoking their own dope'. For instance, when they behave in ways that are reminiscent of their past, we might say, 'But they *see* life in a deeper, more clear and aware state than we mere mortals.' If we think that, it is the beginning of the end. That is the start of 'cultism' and the sign of our 'lostness'.

Our beliefs may be true for us or true for those in our field of association, but they are never, ever 'the truth', though they're easily and eagerly taken to be so. To live life in the belief that we possess 'the truth' (and, I repeat, that includes everything in this guide or any other book) is living in a state of impossibility.

We never really know 'the ultimate truth'. We may get approximations to what are called physical facts, but anything that relies on our memory is distorted at best or completely incorrect at worst. I hope I am never called to be a witness in a trial that relies on my recollections of something in the past, or that my guilt or innocence depends on another's memory.

Use the material here as a guide, pointing you towards Possibility and what is available to you within that realm, which will, to whatever degree, transform your life.

Some people have read this content and become lost in new belief, opinion, judgement, dogma and impossibility – I have seen this happen many times. Others have been touched by an *insight* or revelation. Their mind clears, they experience a beautiful feeling and a buoyancy and lightness never known to them before. They realise that what is occurring is within their mind and has nothing to do with anyone else, and that their experience is normal and natural and available to anyone whose mind clears from the illusion they live in.

My point is that, while not lying or wanting to mislead you, if you take anything that I say as 'the truth', you will fail to *see* the central – actually the only – point of this book. Possibility is not 'the truth', something fossilised that can be held on to. I am simply pointing towards clarity, Possibility and renewal. I am pointing you towards your freedom from belief and from your need to believe.

I USED TO THINK I WAS OPEN, AND TOO OFTEN STILL DO

It's both laughable and embarrassing when I think back. And it's a reality check when it happens now, as it still does. It seemed to me that John Wood was an open-minded person. Some might have agreed with my self-assessment. More would have realised how closed I was. Like most, I was blind to my own closed mind.

According to the Collins Dictionary, 'open' means 'not closed or barred; affording free passage, access, view; not blocked or obstructed; not sealed, fastened or wrapped; having the interior part accessible'. This was how I saw my openness.

My wife, Ronnie, had a different view. She often told me I was closed. She also used words like 'inflexible', 'rigid', 'self-opinionated' and 'arrogant' (views shared by others). I didn't *see* what she meant. My life's journey was about being open, as was my work as a counsellor, coach, adviser, teacher and businessman. Where would she find a more open human being?

One morning, while holidaying in our stunning southwest forest country, sitting behind a large picture window, soaking in the early morning sun, it suddenly dawned on me: Ronnie was right! My wife and others had been experiencing something about me that I had been closed to – something that I had previously not *seen*. Finally, I *saw* what she was noticing.

I had an *insight*. I awoke to the previously un*seen*. I had a fresh flow of Thought. I *saw* that I was, rather than being open, merely being *receptive*. Receptive, I *saw* in that moment, was not open but a *deceptive* way of appearing to be open, deceptive both to me and to others. Receptive had, until that moment, looked like open to me. This *insight* hit me hard!

'Receptive': 'able to apprehend quickly; tending to receive new ideas or suggestions favourably; able to hold or receive'. That was me! I apprehended quickly, and received new ideas or suggestions favourably, more often than not. I was able to hold or receive. I was *receptive* when at my best – but no way was I ever truly *open*.

And from where I was now *seeing* myself, the distinction between receptive and open was the distance between Perth and London. I *saw* clearly for the first time that *open* and *receptive* were *totally* unrelated. I understood, in that moment of *seeing* Possibility, how being receptive is us innocently *acting* as if we're open. In fact, this unwitting pretence blocks a person from being truly open. I will flesh out this enigma below.

Receptivity, like openness, is considered in our society to be a positive quality. In reality, being receptive is simply being closed, cloaked in nice, friendly, urbane packaging. A nice smile and a warm disposition can give the appearance of openness.

We can easily convince ourselves that we know 'the truth' of who we are – for years, even a lifetime – and fail to engage with life from The Realm of Possibility and genuine openness to Life.

DISTINGUISHING BETWEEN OPENNESS AND RECEPTIVITY

The following three vignettes look at being **closed**, being **receptive** and then being **open** in a conversation around the value of thinking strategically in marketing.

I'm not saying you must be open. I am saying that to *see* Possibility you, of necessity, have to be open, and being so is a lot trickier than it might seem.

Phil, a marketing consultant and strategic planner, wants to 'deliver his promise' to Western Engineering. He is convinced of his own expertise, adamant that he has the key to Western Engineering becoming even more successful than it currently is.

James, the CEO at Western Engineering, is a very experienced and successful businessman. He also has an aversion to consultants.

Phil is first depicted in a *closed*, then *receptive* and finally in an *open* state.

CLOSED (PHIL NOT ABLE TO *SEE* POSSIBILITY)

James – the potential client: 'I just can't see how spending money on advertising at this time of year will give us a return. Our best sales are made in summer, not in the middle of winter. It's dead quiet. I can't justify the expenditure – it will be a waste of money!'

Phil – the potential consultant – is three years out of university with his MA marketing degree. He is doing well in his chosen profession but reacts to such thinking from a potential client: 'Well, James, I've learnt from the best on how to think and strategically plan marketing programs to build a brand and grow sales. I understand how I can help you. I've already helped several companies move to the top of the pile in their respective markets.'

In this far-from-exaggerated exchange, Phil is reacting to such a challenge to his expertise. It probably also shows the sensitivity of his young age to being rebuffed. His reply is adversarial. He has instantly turned the exchange into a debate. The discourse is likely to escalate into him being shown the door, rather than a conversation where ideas are explored. Phil is <u>closed</u>: his ability to engage, to listen, to explore when met with a snub is zero. Game, set, match.

He will leave having discovered nothing new about how James sees business, marketing, advertising, and strategic thinking. More importantly, he will have failed to discover why James is so successful without the apparent benefit of strategic thinking in marketing and brand building.

The next example shows how being *receptive* can look like being *open* but is just a clever camouflage, hiding being *closed*.

RECEPTIVE (PHIL STILL NOT ABLE TO *SEE* POSSIBILITY)

To the same reaction from James, Phil says, under the deceptive guise of openness: 'Well, James, I have had the same response from company owners many times. I am really open to and interested in what you have to say. But let me tell you first how I've already helped several companies get to the top of the pile in their respective markets with the strategies I have in mind for you.'

In this example, Phil seems, on the surface, much less defensive – even suggesting he is open to James's point of view. You might say he is receptive to an open conversation and discussion. His tone and words are not adversarial; rather, more engaging. He is inviting James to consider his point of view and is even asking for more input from James – but later.

Phil, in this example, shows he is a skilled conversationalist, but behind the scenes his mind is made up. He is pretending to be open and engaging, but despite his pleasant, urbane response, Phil's mind is closed. He is convinced (he knows for certain) that his understanding of strategic thinking around marketing is best for James's business. He is wanting to prove his point. He is not genuinely looking to explore with an open mind, from The Realm of Possibility, what James knows – and discover why he is such a successful businessperson.

Phil, because he is holding tight his beliefs around his reality, will discover nothing new about James. Phil's thinking (as in the first example of being 'closed') is caught in the trap of knowing (being right) and ultimately disagreeing and making James wrong.

This distinction can be subtle and hard to *see*, as all of us, at least some of the time, are just like Phil.

Again, I'm not suggesting it's compulsory to be open. If, however, we want to *see* Possibility and be successful in our relationships, then being *truly open* is the gateway.

OPEN (TO *SEEING* POSSIBILITY)

The acid test as to whether we are open or not is whether we are evaluating, judging, comparing, rating what another is saying or whether we are simply taking their ideas in and allowing them to be.

Finally, to the same reaction from James, Phil intentionally releases his convictions around strategic planning and marketing. He puts them aside, as it were. Now, this can be very challenging to do, but with practice and the intention, it can be done. Remember that *seeing* Possibility is the potential reward.

With authentic neutrality, Phil says: 'James, I'm interested in what you know around business and how it is that you've been so successful. Tell me your secret. That is, if you are willing to share that with me.'

Phil, in this conversation, is <u>genuinely</u> not interested in what he thinks he knows. He is open to knowing what James knows and thinks. He puts his intention into not knowing and really listening to James. The conversation flows, with James explaining to Phil why he has been successful in business. Phil continues to ask James questions, seeking more information about what James knows. Phil is not trying to find any weakness in James's position. He simply wants to learn – to discover what he doesn't know.

Phil does not give any information on how or why what he has to offer might be helpful, unless asked by James to do so, and Phil will then do so only if he *sees* that James really wants to know what he might think (i.e. is open) rather than just being polite.

Phil's interest is sincere in finding out how James sees business. He is not pushing his own barrow and has nothing on his mind other than holding the intention of listening deeply to James. Phil is completely open to discoveries around the value of what James knows about business and, as importantly, about James the person. What makes him tick.

This conversation between Phil and James is not about agreement, disagreement or even different points of view. The first two conversations were, although the second was in a disguised form, with Phil being deceptively receptive.

This third conversation is, rather, an exploration by Phil of the unknown – James's view on business. Also facilitated by Phil's questions is an exploration by James of his own reality.

Nor is this conversation about agreement. Phil's position is one of neutrality and discovery – not knowing. He is coming to the conversation from The Realm of Possibility – to the best he can in each moment of the conversation.

This doesn't mean Phil will give up his intention of working with James. It doesn't mean he will get James's business. It doesn't mean he has to defend being an exponent of strategic thinking in marketing and advertising.

It doesn't mean anything other than he is truly open to *seeing what is* on the other side of (i.e. beyond) his own thinking around his view of business to this point.

So, being closed is being closed. Being receptive might mean listening to the words someone is saying with attention, even with good grace, but not fooling yourself into thinking you are open. Behind the scenes, our mind is stuck in opinions, judgements and/or evaluative ideas about what is being said, based on the intention of getting a deal.

No matter what our beliefs are, we cannot be having them – or judgements – about what someone is saying and at the same time be open to them, their ideas and, more to the point, open to Possibility.

Being open means we allow free passage, access; our mind is not blocked or obstructed – our interior is accessible. These are the key aspects that make the clear distinction between *receptive* and *open*. In holding, even feather-lightly, the hidden opinion, 'I don't agree', even though we may appear receptive, we are closed to what is being said (because we hold an opinion).

And again, don't be fooled. If we hold the opinion, 'I agree', to what is being said, we are equally closed because we are judging what is being said with a concurring belief or opinion. We are simply colluding with the other person's view.

SOME POPULAR MENTAL-TRAINING MODELS AND POSSIBILITY

Techniques based on re-programming our subconscious mind (an aspect of memory) keep us mired in conditioning.

Our number-one habit is being stuck in habitual thinking. This problem extends to mental-training models – even ones intended to liberate us from bad habits in our thinking.

This guide isn't about receiving more training, although some un-training (as in the Realm of Possibility Workshop, outlined in Appendix 2) will assist, so long as it doesn't end up creating more habitual thinking.

There are important distinctions between Possibility and some popular forms of mind work. First and foremost, Possibility *isn't positive thinking*. Clear and inspired thinking will automatically *result* from *seeing* Possibility. *Seeing* Possibility is unlikely to occur when intentionally practising positive-thinking techniques.

Possibility is *seen* in a state of awareness – it is not evoked by a technique. In that realm of awareness, we experience extraordinary clarity, a sense of deep calm and an unshakable positivity around whatever original or fresh view is *seen* – even if what is *seen* foretells trouble ahead. Within the Realm of Possibility, we can *see* creation and, equally, destruction, things improving or things going 'to hell in a hand basket'. But whatever we *see*, the same mental freedom, clarity and calm exist. We *see* destruction with the same clarity as we *see* creation. Clarity of thinking around every aspect of our daily life results from *seeing* Possibility.

PRACTISING POSITIVE THINKING TAKES EFFORT

Positive thinking is promoted by those who haven't experienced Possibility, or by those who don't understand what it is when they have.

As it is usually described, positive thinking is a process for, and a result of, trying to train or discipline our mind to think more positively. At best, it is the impetus for a change in our conditioning, a change from some habitual negative or less-than-helpful thought patterns. That can be all well and good, but it is still not transformation. At best, it is re-programming – developing different and hopefully better habitual thinking. This can be extremely useful in increasing our competence in areas where we need to hone a specific skill.

Seeing Possibility, however, is the antithesis of training. It enables us to *see* our programming for what it is. We are no longer wedded to our thinking, positive or otherwise.

Positive thinking has, in my view, limited staying power. You will always need to be 'working on it' to sustain your positive momentum. Nor, as I understand them, are techniques like NLP (Neuro-Linguistic Programming), affirmation, creative visualisation, prayer, or any other model or process being offered, related to Possibility.

Techniques based on re-programming our subconscious mind (an aspect of memory) keep us mired in additional conditioning. We already have layers of overly conditioned, programmed beliefs to *see* through if we are to experience a state of fresh Thought. Does adding further layers make sense?

From extensive reading, experimentation and training in NLP, affirmation and visualisation during my 30s and early 40s – and from having been a trainer in them – my understanding is that these processes are about imprinting ideas into our subconscious mind through various techniques, including ongoing repetition. They are about embedding ideas in our memory, creating a pattern of thinking that supplants, overrides, improves or changes the existing one/s. Each is a form of conditioning, the very aspect of our mental state beyond which we need to *see* to experience Possibility. While improved conditioning it may be, it is still mental clutter that blocks *seeing* Possibility.

But let me strongly qualify what I am saying here about NLP, visualisation or any other similar technique you might be familiar with. Many elite athletes and performers of all types use those techniques to improve skills and hone performance. Correctly applied, such techniques will work, embedding important habits that will benefit performance.

These techniques will help greatly, for example, in playing the piano well – maybe to concert level. But when it comes to composing an original piece of music, except for providing the technical platform, all learning is subordinate to fresh Thought: it is fresh, original Thought that creates the new melody, lyrics, and musical interpretation.

Memory provides our predisposition to certain music and enables us to put it on paper and recall it as needed. Possibility is the source of an 'original score'. *Seeing* Possibility is *seeing* beyond our memories, beyond our subconscious and the accumulations of our lifetime. It's hearing beyond the last melody or creative idea we experienced to be able to access a new one. It is *seeing* an entirely new (never even considered) use for an old product, or building, or organisation, or skill set.

While training-based approaches have many advocates, practitioners and students worldwide, none of them is aligned, so far as I *see*, with *seeing* Possibility, creativity or originality.

Seeing Possibility is not a technique, it is not a skill, it cannot be learned. It is a naturally occurring function of being human, available to any mind that in the moment is willing to be free of the past, to *see*. It occurs in a mind that can observe itself thinking and not taking that thinking as 'the truth'.

CHAPTER 3

HOW POSSIBILITY CAN WORK IN ANY BUSINESS OR ORGANISATION

When looking at life through our lens of beliefs, opinions, judgements, knowledge and experience, we forgo seeing *Possibility.*

In a state of lightly held views (remaining unrestrained, unrestricted, and unimpeded by those views) we can, if we so desire, reflect on anything we think important: our business or creative pursuits, a relationship, our health, life in general, sustainability, our career – whatever aspect/s of our life we care passionately about.

We can reflect anywhere: working at a hobby, lying in bed, having a shower or going for a run. It can be in the hubbub of city life or the tranquillity of a secret hideaway. Today, for me, it was lying back in my dentist's chair. The place is of no consequence. Possibility exists for us anywhere, everywhere and at any time we give up our attachment to our beliefs, opinions, judgements and knowledge and surrender to the unknown.

It is not for us to visualise, affirm, imagine, pray for, meditate on, or do anything with the idea dear to us. Gently cradle it for as long as it stays in your mind. Recall it as and when you want to, or as it involuntarily pops back into your mind.

For example, take a person who wants to start their own engineering business. How might *seeing* Possibility allow them to carry out that desire?

One way is for them to put the idea on a low flame and let it simmer in the back of their mind. They should maintain just enough energy to keep it warm. And it can be any idea as to how they can take the first step, as at this point the aim is to let these ideas quietly bubble away in their mind.

If the idea remains relevant (important) to them, it will recur time and time again. They will gradually, or quite quickly in some cases, have all sorts of other ideas around that central idea. Possibility will deliver to them ideas about how they might go about achieving their desired outcome.

And they may also think of how impossible it is to achieve their goals. How they don't have the resources, time, contacts, funds, knowledge, business experience, etc. to get the project up and running. This type of thinking will also most likely come to mind. That's okay. It is also possible that what they contemplate may spawn different ideas that are even more important and relevant to them. If the first idea doesn't keep coming to mind, it's no longer a priority. Trying to force or control our thinking is of no use, in fact quite counterproductive to *seeing* into The Realm of Possibility. If the idea of having their own engineering business truly holds their fascination, fresh ideas will come to mind as to how they might start.

My idea of having my own caravan business materialised with a very old, nine-foot mini-caravan purchased for peanuts. It was what I could afford and could manage, and my dad and I set about renovating it on the driveway of our home. The scale of the goal didn't influence our starting point. We just took one miniscule step.

What happens to us when we *see* Possibility is that we *see* a step we can take in the direction of our vision, then another, and another, and so on. This is the process (quick or slow) of a yet-to-be-*seen* reality, which in its own good time becomes clear in our mind's eye as a partially or fully formed vision. The idea is *seen*, in enough form for us to act, to start creating our heart's desire, whatever that may be. And it's fun. It's exciting. It's Possibility unfolding in our personal reality.

We each move in our own way. But when reflecting on something seemingly out of reach, just observe any thoughts of impossibility or limitation. Just enjoy reflecting on and considering any ideas from The Realm of Possibility that might come to mind. Who knows what ideas may arise if you want to create your own engineering business. You may *see* that starting from your home workshop is an important step in the direction of your vision. Possibility is in action. Who knows what we will *see* next, once action has taken place and we are witnessing a new reality.

Understand, though, that we have no control when we enter The Realm of Possibility. What we *see* is out of our hands. Possibility is *seen* when we move into a not-knowing, innocent state of awareness. At that point all our beliefs, opinions and judgements will be *seen* simply as ideas that we hold, and not as the stifling 'truth' that once blinded our view to that deeper reality.

HOW DO WE *SEE* POSSIBILITY?

For me, it occurs like this:

- An idea comes to mind that I am fascinated by, feel motivated by (for example: how can I start an engineering business?).
- This idea may have come out of the blue, or it might have been triggered by reading something, or being told about something, but I don't *see* it in its complete form.
- I play with the idea, tinker with it, toss it around in my mind.
- I don't want to let it go. It seems too important.
- The idea persists, and might do so for an hour, day, week, month, year or more. In the case of the Realm of Possibility Project, it has been, in various forms, popping into my mind for several decades. I didn't have a name for it. I just wanted to share with the world the power of original Thought and the trap of its form – our memory. The Philosophy of Everyday Living Centre was an early form of The Realm of Possibility Project.
- Time is not relevant. I just leave it simmering away.
- *Seeing* a workable way forward is what I am waiting to discover.
- My level of fascination with the idea is what sustains my motivation to realise the vision. This is key.
- Out of the blue, a fresh Thought occurs of how I might engage with and bring the idea to life.
- This 'light-bulb' moment might happen many times in many different ways, but it might not be within my capacity to carry out the 'plan' at that time.
- The way I am looking at it might be too big for me, or just not the right fit at a particular time.
- These ideas *are always* fresh or, if previously experienced, *seen* again as if for the first time and generally in a new way.
- Out of the blue, I then *see* how to begin in a way that makes perfect sense – another 'a-ha' moment along the journey. For example: starting from my home workshop, if I take on small jobs only, will work for me and keep my overheads to a minimum.

- It might not make any sense to anyone else. In fact, it often doesn't (if I'm in a high-paying job and enjoy minimal risk of failure, for example), as those you might talk to about your idea haven't *seen* what you have *seen* so it doesn't seem feasible or it might look downright impossible – even foolish.

- In all probability, I will, if that is still my heart's desire, start immediately carrying out the plan.

- I don't have to; however, if moved to, I will begin.

The examples from my life where I *saw* Possibility all saw the light of day roughly in the way described above. As you read on, the foregoing will, I trust, make increasing sense.

Wifi wonder

In 1977, an Australian electrical engineer called Dr John O'Sullivan was working in a radio observatory in The Netherlands. Along with two colleagues, he wrote a paper on how to improve the clarity of radio-astronomy images. He would later draw on the technological breakthroughs outlined in that paper when, in the 1990s, he led a team at the CSIRO that patented a technique for reducing interference in radio signals in computer networks. Without going into the brain-frying tech specs of it all, suffice to say that this technique revolutionised the speed and reliability of wireless LANs (Local Area Networks). It is now a core component of wifi networks across the globe: the CSIRO has earned over $A500 million in royalties on the patent's use, and considerably more from lawsuits over its illegal use.

Few Australians outside the fields of engineering and computer technology will have heard of O'Sullivan. Yet the world as we know it has been transformed by the expertise of he and his colleagues. It's now wireless everything. Think about it, starting with your phone, your office, your leisure-time streaming service ... his stamp is on so much of our lives, we are hugely indebted to his creative spirit.

He has won numerous awards, including the prestigious European Inventor Award in 2012 (given by the EU) and the Australian Prime Minister's Prizes for Science in 2009.

O'Sullivan used his scientific knowledge to make major advances in radio signalling. He then used Possibility to *see* links between outer space and an office computer network.

The Internet is a breath-taking miracle. Wifi – which has taken connectivity freedom to unimaginable levels – is a life-changing wonder. That's what Possibility can do for us.

OF TWO STATES OF MIND – CONSCIOUS OR UNCONSCIOUS LEADERSHIP

Leadership: surely one of the most admired, condemned, researched, studied, written- and talked-about qualities of we humans.

For me, leadership is a state of mind. If our thinking in the moment is influenced from a state of Possibility, we produce our best, given our present skills and abilities. If not, we do poorly, even if we are highly intelligent and highly experienced, and have extensive training in leadership.

The frames of reference I use are around leaders of business. While the purpose and details of the work of leaders of all other organisations differ from those of the businessperson, all leaders share the essentials, those qualities at the heart of the matter: kindness, understanding, wisdom and common sense.

Our state of awareness determines whether the challenges and opportunities that present themselves will benefit us alone or the broader community as well.

You might say our use of Thought has us engaging with life, either from a self-absorbed perspective, or from a perspective that encompasses the common good.

In my experience, the genuine entrepreneur in a state of Possibility is motivated by much more than making money. S/he *sees* serving others as integral to any project *seen* and undertaken. These are the entrepreneurs demonstrating 'conscious leadership'.

On the other hand, let's look at the 'opportunistic businessperson', or those displaying 'unconscious leadership'. This person taps only their memory, with its storehouse of conditioning (rather than *seeing* Possibility and the vantage point that provides), so they are confined in their vision and their actions to thinking only about their own imagined needs, wants and desires.

In this state of mind, i.e. the realm of impossibility, they are driven by gaining personal advantage. Often it is purely monetary. Sometimes it is the imagined status and power such an opportunity may buy or bring with it, or maybe it's a combination of these or other factors. The opportunist is, by definition, governed by the way they have been conditioned.

An opportunist is unlikely to have been given cause to reflect on the common good growing up. And if their business gives the appearance of being in service to the common good, it is likely that what is being offered is bait for a higher personal reward and/or accolades the opportunist can see coming down the track. Being in service to others (to the common good) is not on that opportunistic businessperson's radar. He or she might be called egocentric.

In a state of Possibility, human beings discount heavily (even if not eliminate entirely) the personal cost/benefit considerations in manifesting the opportunity *seen*. Our powerful drive is moderated by kindness, understanding, wisdom and common sense. We do what we do for the benefit of all, including ourselves.

On the other hand, seeing business from our conditioned state of mind, as an opportunist, we see the personal cost/benefit considerations as being all that matter. The common good is of little – and, in its extreme, of no – consequence in the decisions we make and the actions we take ... decisions that often prove detrimental to the common good.

The collective level of consciousness of a Board of Directors and the CEO is either guided by a state of Possibility or impossibility; we are either a consciously or unconsciously led business or organisation.

In a state of mind influenced by Possibility, corporate decisions are made with the common good in mind. In a state of impossibility, benefits to the corporation dominate the culture, and at the extreme end of the spectrum *only* those that benefit the Board, CEO, and the most senior personnel are considered. Shareholders in this culture are considered only out of the self-interest of the Board. Customers, staff, community and the environment may not figure in their deliberations and decisions. If they do, it is only in terms of how best they can be exploited and used for the benefit of those at the top. You may know of corporations, governments, organisations, including not-for-profits, that fall into this bag.

There is a great price to pay with impossibility leadership, but the costs are not *seen* when the decisions are made. If they were, those decisions would not be made.

Globally, the last three decades or so have been dominated by impossibility thinking at the most senior levels. These decades have seen opportunistic thinking playing out in the boardrooms of companies and parliaments around the world. Results include the Global Financial Crisis and the parlous state the world is in today, ethically, economically, environmentally, politically and socially.

LEADING BY LISTENING

We *see* to the heart of the matter when we genuinely listen to another.

Listening in this way has everything to do with the other, and nothing to do with the other. It has everything to do with us, and nothing to do with us.

Authentic listening takes us beyond the distortions of our mental accumulation – our beliefs, opinions, judgements and knowledge.

In this state of clarity, we understand the other from a state of Possibility. We are hearing beyond the words expressed – exploring the 'authentic self' in them and the 'authentic self' in ourselves.

This quality of listening informs us when we are missing the deeper meaning behind the words used by the other.

This level of listening prompts questions from our state of Possibility, rather than assumptions from our conditioned mind. We are able if we intend to deepen mutual understanding, to use these questions to explore the hidden reality behind the words expressed.

If we are indeed truly listening, we will 'listen the other into being their authentic self'. We hear *their* meaning, *not our own*, behind the words they are using.

In summary: If we, out of ingrained habit, and without realising, attribute our meaning to what the other is saying, what we hear is no more than a reflection of what we think and mean. Instead, if we are perceptively listening, we are searching for what *they* believe, and thus what *they* truly mean.

When we listen in this way, a miracle occurs – the other person comes to understand themselves. And we come to understand them and ourselves in this mutual process of discovery.

A wondrous meeting of two minds occurs.

ENTREPRENEURIAL THINKING VS OPPORTUNISTIC THINKING (CONSCIOUS VS UNCONSCIOUS LEADERSHIP)

Authentic entrepreneurialism recognises the common good – opportunism is limited to feeding our false self.

What follows illustrates the distinctions between the two states of mind: one of Possibility and conscious leadership, or another of impossibility and unconscious leadership. As said, this applies to everyone, for we are all leaders of a kind. The two columns below signify when you and I are leading from one state or the other.

Authentic Power	Inauthentic Power
We *see* that power is inherent within all human beings, emanating from within our mind. We don't experience power as being externally generated by others over us or us over others. Life is not seen as a power game, as winning or losing, but of you and me free of ego, allowing Possibility to reveal the best way forward and direct our individual actions. We understand that no person, group or way of looking at life holds 'the truth'. We realise that authentic power resides at our core, within every human being, and manifests in kindness, understanding, wisdom and common sense.	We believe power is external to ourselves, residing in education, societal structures, rank, affiliation, social standing, image and money. Inauthentic power focuses on trying to control what others think and do. Power over others and over circumstances preoccupies our thinking and exhausts our energy. Life is a never-ending striving for advantage. Winning, getting our way and exercising power and control over others is what matters to us above all else.
Fearlessness	Fearfulness
With the source of fear *seen* as coming from within our mind, our leadership is not ruled by imagined, fearful, or reactive thinking. The distinction between psychological fear born in past experiences and the actual threat of a real and present danger is clearly *seen*. In that *seeing*, our fear becomes an appropriate, helpful emotion, rather than an overwhelming psychological burden that controls and drives our actions.	Since we are unaware of the internal source of fear, our survival seems constantly under threat from others and from fluctuating circumstances. Our fearful thinking drives us to seek the imagined security that the illusion of power and control provides. Being blind to the power of our beliefs, opinions, and judgements has them driving and controlling us. Our lack of understanding blinds us to *seeing* through our fear to fresh Thought and Possibility.

Authentic Listening	Pretend Listening
Listening to others deeply and respectfully (without our beliefs, opinions and judgements over-riding our *seeing what is*) is a treasured experience. Our listening powerfully facilitates drawing out the authentic thinking, feelings and creative ideas both within ourselves and in others. At our deeper level of listening, we encourage the separate and differing realities of others to be expressed, explored and considered. In this state of authentic listening we hear clearly what we may feel uncomfortable with. Differences are not threatening to us. Our listening provides the environment in which others might also *see* Possibility.	At best, we pretend to listen. Using BS phrases like 'I hear you,' we hear the words but are untouched by the thinking or feelings behind them. Unaware (even temporarily) of the authentic individual within others, and ourselves, we are disconnected, threatened and reactive to difference. At worst, we don't even pretend to listen; we ignore, and in our fear-based arrogance, ride roughshod over others. Our lack of listening holds impossibility in place for ourselves, and fosters a fearful environment.
In Integrity	Out of Integrity
We are in integrity with our inner kindness, understanding, wisdom and common sense. Our connection with our deeper intelligence and inner authority enables us to hold steady in the face of extreme difficulty. Short-term solutions and gains are not sought. The distinctions between what is sustainable and unsustainable are obvious to us.	We vacillate, give in to pressure and keep changing our mind under what we experience as external pressure. We have little sense of *what is* real and what is false. Expediency, self-preservation and the need for personal power and the illusion of personal control rule us. We are blindly committed to 'the party line', as we imagine it serves us even when the greater good isn't served by it.
Vanguards and Champions	Self-Promoters
We are vanguards for what will benefit others, the common good and the planet. We are champions for the advancement of our colleagues, our community and humanity, and demonstrate courage and humility in doing so. Those we support could be near or in far-off lands; it makes no difference.	We promote ourselves and seek power, wealth, glory and fame, either directly or through some proxy. Exploiting others is our *modus operandi*. We cannot genuinely support others and promote life-enhancing causes because our narcissism and need to be in the limelight drive us.
Independent Thinking	Second-Guessing
We are independent while simultaneously being genuine team players, providing the team outcome is in service to the common good. For us, toe-ing the party line when we *see* that it is not serving the common good and being mindlessly involved and supporting the	We lead by second-guessing those we see as pulling the strings, from opinion polls, by selling out to pressure groups, or by our need to be part of the control group. Our access to fresh Thought, inner wisdom and common sense is constantly overridden by

unsupportable and unsustainable are anathema. We make decisions based on our inner wisdom and integrity even when pressured to support or vote with the so-called power group.	our fear and conditioning. Independent and original Thought is forgotten territory; the power-line is our line. We blindly follow or go along to get along.
Free	A Prisoner
In accessing Possibility we are: - free to *see* and explore creative and innovative ideas – ours or others'; - free to *see* the obvious – to *see what is*, rather than being ruled by our ideas, beliefs, opinions and judgements; - free to *see* beyond the 'wisdom of the day'; - free to explore ideas and solutions put forward by others even though they may not make sense to us; - free to *see* our allies and our opponents with equal clarity, objectivity, kindness, understanding, wisdom and common sense.	In failing to access Possibility, we see only what we have been conditioned to see. The obvious has become invisible to us. We don't see *what is*. In that state of mind we are blocking our access to fresh Thought, and experience life exactly as it conforms to our conditioned thinking. We spend our life manipulating and conniving; doing whatever it takes to get our neurotic (and, in the extreme, sociopathic or psychopathic) needs met and to survive. Consolidating and furthering our imagined needs, wants and desires is our solitary confinement.
Connection to Life	Disconnection from Life
We experience a reverence for Life in all its manifestations. The distinction between 'them' and 'us' fades – eventually to extinction. The notions of tolerance and acceptance are transcended by our kind understanding and embrace.	We don't experience a reverence for Life because we don't experience being part of it. We feel separate, imagine we are superior, and use, abuse, and dispense with people. We exploit nature and, as a result, pollute the earth, waterways and air. Overwhelmed by our own need for survival, we're numb to the deeper feelings and connection with Life. Possibility lies dormant within.
Faith	Lack of or Misplaced Faith
A faith in the wonder and mystery of Life translates to faith in our self, our colleagues, and the world of Possibility that we *see* as innate within all humanity. Notwithstanding some of the impossibility thinking and behaviour around us, we *see* that all humanity is, at its essence, Possibility.	Any faith we may have is based on an external authority, deity, ideology or belief system.

Loyalty	Loyalty is Missing
Seeing Possibility enables us to transcend the ever-changing circumstances life throws up. We remain loyal to our relationships. Even when difficult decisions, such as firing subordinates, are to be made, we have the best interests of our colleagues at heart and the common good in mind. Trust in our leadership and in our integrity is seldom doubted, even in times of great disruption and despair.	Noble feelings, including loyalty, are missing from our daily experience and therefore our leadership. This lack of loyalty manifests in many ways and contributes to the distrust and anxiety permeating our organisation. It is always a case of me – first, second, and …
Being Ordinary	Being Special
Seeing from the vantage point of Possibility allows us to recognise the extraordinary range, skill and depth of qualities and abilities within humanity. We also recognise our own uniqueness, strengths and weaknesses. In accessing Possibility, we *see* the sublime everywhere and, in that context, recognise our own ordinariness in the grand scheme of Life.	In failing to *see* Possibility, we are blind to the wonderful qualities in others and in ourselves. We think that being special, being the best, and being in control will fill our need to feel worthwhile.
Awake to Life	Asleep at the Wheel of Life
We are awake to our moment-to-moment experience, whatever that may be – what we might describe as good, bad or indifferent, arising within our mind. We *see* our life as an ever-unfolding process, creative or otherwise, or one that simply recycles our past, at best with some minor renovations and additions. We recognise that the degree to which we are awake equates to our capacity in the moment to *see* Possibility more clearly via accessing fresh Thought. We are conscious of how Possibility or impossibility shapes our moment-to-moment thinking, feelings and behaviour.	We experience life as something that is happening outside of us and to us. We are sleeping within the illusion of yesterday's Thought-created reality and imagine the dream is real today. In our failure to *see what is*, we feel frightened, jumping at the shadows cast by our own thinking.
A Love Affair with Life	A Love Affair with Ourselves
We regularly experience our life beyond our knowledge, beliefs, opinions, judgements, ideologies and dogmas. We have tasted the experience of unconditional love. We know that quality of love that exists within The Realm of Possibility. As a result, we are in love with life and all that Life represents.	Our predominant state is self-absorption. Romance, sex, excitement, infatuation, idealism and all manner of good intentions are possible for us, but uncontaminated, unconditional, and therefore uncontained love from The Realm of Possibility is impossible in our self-involved state. Our love affair is with our self – our beliefs, opinions, judgements and knowledge.

Our Priorities are Aligned and Congruent	Our Priorities Conflict
Within the context of wisdom and common sense, we *see* and understand *'what really works'*. This leads to: - delivering the promise to clients, staff and shareholders; - thinking strategically; - fiscal prudence; - sound organisation and administration; - productive effort; - self-discipline; - self-responsibility; - carefully considered risk-taking. Within the context of kindness and understanding, we *see* and understand *'what really matters'*. This leads to: - having a vision and purpose that transcends the individual and addresses the needs of the common good; - fairness, decency and equity; - fostering and supporting the aspirations of others; - sustainability in resource use, of the environment, health and the wellbeing of all; - caring for those that cannot care for themselves. In understanding how the convergence of *'what actually works'* with *'what actually matters,'* our leadership both works and matters. We lead by example with a minimalist approach to all forms of power and control. We don't tell people what they should and shouldn't do; we *see* that they too have access to Possibility and the kindness,	We think our beliefs, opinions and judgements are right and that others are wrong in theirs. We 'know' our depth and breadth of knowledge is superior. We don't recognise that doing *'what works'* or doing *'what matters'* in isolation from one another and in separate silos of ideological thinking, fails sooner or later. Driven and controlled by our conditioning, we lead rigidly from impossibility thinking – the power and control mentality of the extremes of left and right. For example, we leaders with beliefs to the 'right' of the political spectrum claim that we have the answers. We claim we know *'what works'* in business and in society more broadly, and if others do what we say works, then that *'works best* and *matters most'*. Of that we have no doubt. We leaders on the 'left' are certain we have the answers to what ails our organisations and society in general. We claim we know *'what matters'* in organisations and in society, and that *if others do what we say matters, that works best for all*. Of that we have no doubt. And we leaders who claim the 'centre' are convinced that we have the answers to the problems the world faces. We believe we have the correct balance between *'what we think works'* and *'what we think matters.'* We, like the left and the right, also fail to understand that conscious leadership is neither about balance nor about any ideology, but rather about working from a state of awareness of Possibility – a state of kindness, understanding, wisdom and common sense.

understanding, wisdom and common sense needed to make sustainable decisions. Our job as a leader is to support a creative, self-reliant but inter-dependent environment.

In *seeing what is,* we are free of a fixed position, we make sound, sustainable decisions and take appropriate action. It may be considered right-wing or left-wing; that is of no consequence.

AND it is reviewing and re-evaluating the situation and taking whatever corrective steps need to be taken.

We are Congruent	We are Incongruent
What we think, what we are feeling, what we say and how we act – all line up. We are authentic in how we show up in the world.	When questioned carefully and closely, we become confused as to what we really think, as we are disconnected from how we feel and speak and act in ways that confuse others as to where we really stand as a human being. Being authentic is foreign to us.

In summary, I *see* a world in which you and I live from Possibility; a world in which we, as businesspeople and as human beings, are kind to and understanding of each other – where our collective wisdom, common sense, sense of fairness and decency govern all our decisions.

I *see* a world where *doing what works* and *doing what matters* seamlessly converge, leading to a state where our actions concerning the Earth and all that live on, below and above her, are sustainable.

'TEAM'-BUILDING

*'The master of the art of living makes little distinction between his
work and his play, his labour and his leisure,
his mind and his body, his education and his recreation,
his love and his religion. He hardly knows which is which;
he simply pursues his vision of excellence in whatever
he does, leaving others to decide whether he is working
or playing. To him he is always doing both.'*

BUDDHA

Within the state of impossibility, there isn't any more debilitating thinking than that of fear. The following material fleshes out how fear can be fostered and too often perpetuated under the guise of 'team-building'.

With the number of team-building or team-development programs run across the planet each year, one could imagine that organisations are populated by cohesive, creative, productive, empowered groups of people – i.e. by teams focused on developing and achieving the Vision, Purpose, Aim, Mission, Goals and Objectives of the organisation (or re-setting them if they are no longer relevant or if they fail to serve the common good). In the process, they feel good about themselves, each other and their clients, and are contributing to their fellow humans' wellbeing. In short, these organisations are living, symbiotic systems committed to the common good.

That is clearly not the case. Talk in confidence with board members, senior management, middle managers and line workers of many organisations, and you will find that many individuals do not in any way feel part of the team. More revealing still, many feel alienated from those they work with, subordinate to and alienated from the organisation that employs them. In the light of your own experience and what you have read thus far, why do you think that is the case?

IS IT TEAM-BUILDING OR SOMETHING ELSE?

'Culture eats strategy for breakfast.'

PETER DRUCKER

Why is it that so many organisational team-building programs fail to deliver the promise?

Why, not long after the training, does team spirit so often take a tumble?

And why, at the mention of the latest team-building initiative, is cynicism and reluctance to engage so prevalent?

The answer, I believe, is this: in programs that do fail there is a common, discernible thread. The incumbent leader's motives (often hidden from him or herself) are to manipulate staff into compliance rather than actually foster a team of inspired, independent, interdependent personalities. Individuals who coalesce for the common good of the team, the organisation and the community.

Why do we, under the guise of building cohesive, creative and innovative teams, harbour – I suspect mostly unconsciously – the intention of creating compliance, agreement and conformity? Many of us are looking for people to do our bidding, rather than looking for those we engage with to be part of a creative, productive and, more importantly, sustainable team of inspired individuals.

This may come as a shock to some readers, particularly to some leaders. It was shocking to me that day, many years ago, when I woke in a state of Possibility to the fact that I, quite unknowingly, fell into that category.

It was an even greater shock when I tried to think of leaders within the sphere of my life that actually encouraged authentic team development. Leaders with the clarity of mind and the internal fortitude to give up their need for power, control, regulation, restraint and in being the 'thought police'. To be an equal among equals. I could recall only a handful.

I don't say there weren't more, just that I had not encountered leaders that I could say embodied the qualities that facilitated team cohesion – that fostered the qualities of fearlessness, authenticity, a unique capacity for deep listening and human understanding as discussed in the earlier section, 'Of Two States of Minds – Conscious or Unconscious Leadership'.

Why is it that so many leaders end up coercing their people into agreement, compliance and dependence rather than engagement, independence, unconventionality and freedom of spirit?

The answer, I think, is surprisingly simple, so simple that you might easily dismiss it out of hand; and it might be so close to home that you stop reading this guide. The human fact is that a high percentage of us live our lives ruled by fear, our life experience dominated by insecure thinking. We inhabit – un*seen* by us – the realm of impossibility on a day-to-day basis.

Look to your first-hand experience of how pervasive and dominant fear is in the workplace – at all levels, including within the leadership. Look within your own mind. As a consequence of experiencing so much fear, people long for security. We look for security in all sorts of places: especially within religious belief, within family, within professional affiliation, within like-minded groups and among friends.

We vote for those we think will protect and promote our interests, our values, our financial future and our cultural heritage. And at work, we try to build teams that will take care of our best interests within the power structures of the organisations we belong to. Fear, not love, is the strong driver throughout society.

CHANGE WITHOUT CHANGING

Learned insecurity (impossibility thinking) is at cause as to why many so-called team-building programs fail to build teams, to create excellence, and to achieve what is innate, but largely inactive, within participants. The un*seen* intention of the training runs contrary to what most, if not all, of us are anticipating, long for and would benefit from. We are looking for something that will help us grow, be the catalyst for us to become more secure, more confident and independent, and at the same time become a more connected, contributing, interdependent part of the team.

What we find is quite different. If not at the time of the program, then certainly later, many of us feel like a disempowered pawn in someone else's game – the game in which the structure must support the ego of our leader. The program, rather than being set up for the common good, is set up for the good of the leadership. When push comes to shove, we leaders are more often than not (and quite innocently) trying to do the following:

- Build a team that will take care of us, our needs and interests.
- Create an environment in which our team will do our bidding without giving us a difficult time.
- Create a climate in which our employees or subordinates will go along with us even when our thinking and decisions are poor.

- Blindly cooperate with us when we are taking the group in a direction that is not in the best interests of the organisation, the team and the common good, and will probably end in disaster.

Sound familiar?

Many leaders fool ourselves when we say: 'I want a team of leaders who will innovate, challenge, question me and take the initiative.' If we meant what we said, we would indeed witness team-building programs that inspire those qualities. Rather, our thinking is dominated by seeking the illusion of safety, sought through acquiring a team of followers, supporters, cheerleaders, good guys and girls who will basically do as they're told and make life easy for us.

So what is the alternative? The answer is obvious! Each page of this guide has been pointing in its direction. It is simple when we *see* it, and as simple – yet challenging – to implement the solution. For us to be a leader who actually builds a team is to be the leader who lives without fear – or at least one who *sees* and understands fear for the imposter it is, and not have it rule our life and ruin our leadership. Leading beyond fear allows for the following:

- **Space** – the psychological, philosophical space in which we and others too can grow, evolve and thrive.

- **Empowerment** – each of us is empowered when free of our conditioned fears. We automatically foster the inherent power that can lie dormant in others.

- **Authenticity and congruence** – again, to be authentic is to be fearless, and being fearless is to be empowered. How often do we hear our political, business, religious and media leaders speak in a way that reeks of inauthenticity, of fear, of disempowerment? It has become the norm. It is certainly common in my homeland, Australia.

- **Listening skills** – a quality of listening that fosters freedom and thus empowerment in both the listener and the speaker. We don't and can't listen when we are fearful. Poor listening is the most obvious sign of disempowerment, just as deep listening is the most obvious sign of empowerment.

- **Understanding** – a clear understanding of our own humanity. Only in understanding ourselves can we understand others. Empowerment comes from that understanding. We *see* that within the reality of *seeing what is*, there is nothing and never was anything to fear. That fear exists in our minds. It is a product of our conditioning – the home of impossibility, and not a product of what is going on in our environment, circumstances, organisation or any of the countless factors to which we attribute our fear.

For team-building to work, fear needs to be *seen* and understood for what it is. It needs to be recognised for the faulty thinking it is, and be *seen* through to be overcome. Fear at every level – at board level, senior-management level and within the ranks – is an imagined construct of each individual's thinking that becomes group thinking that stymies the organisation.

The question is this: how do we *see* fear as the illusion we create in our minds and, in so doing, move beyond it? We overcome fear when we *see* with clarity and with certainty the genesis of fear. We overcome fear when we *see* that fear is a product of our thinking – and not a fact of life created by our surroundings or circumstances.

The degree to which we realise that fear is something we have learnt growing up (being recalled in the moment from memory as a habit of our thinking), and is not a result of what is currently presenting, will determine to the exact same degree whether we experience fearlessness. We become increasingly fearless the more we *see* the illusory nature of our thinking (and therefore the illusory nature of fear). This understanding is a shift in our awareness – a shift in our level of consciousness from disempowerment to empowerment.

Fear and fear alone sabotages us building a team.

Fearlessness is sufficient in and of itself to enable genuine team-building to occur. It is that simple. Fearlessness is *seeing what is,* not what we imagine it to be.

To understand the genesis of team building and address the common source of fear, to foster safety and build sustainable organisations performing at peak levels, free of stress and worry, The Realm of Possibility Workshop (see Appendix 2) is a good next step you might want to consider taking, perhaps offering it to your executive group in-house.

And there is no aspect of the human experience more transparent in revealing the prevailing states of mind than in the way businesses and organisations function at the individual and collective level. The following chapter looks into what is behind success, mediocrity and failure in businesses and organisations. Intuitively I recognised this back in my Fleetwood days; however, with no understanding of what was going on in my mind or the minds of others, it was four steps forward and three-and-a-half back.

THE FOURTH ELEMENT OF BUSINESS AND ORGANISATION: THOUGHT

> *'The world we have made, as a result of the level of thinking we have done so far, creates problems we cannot solve at the same level at which we created them.'*
>
> ALBERT EINSTEIN

A critically important area of society in which fresh ideas constantly occur is in business and organisation. Within that context of businesses and organisations (no matter how big or small), I call Thought and its product, our moment-to-moment thinking, 'The Fourth Element of Business and Organisation'. What follows is a discussion of how Thought (fresh or in its conditioned state) makes or breaks businesses and organisations.

For simplicity's sake, in defining and exploring the Fourth Element, I distinguish it from all of the well-known and equally well-understood components of business and organisations. I have grouped these familiar components together as three other elements: skills, systems and finance.

AWAY WITH THE FAIRIES, OR SWAPPING IDEAS?

Some years back, I was having lunch with Barry Urquhart, an old friend and colleague and a much-respected international business consultant and author. There was collegial warmth and respect between Barry and myself, but even so, the concept of Possibility I was putting forward took an initial beating!

Explaining the un*seen* was tough. Nevertheless I made my pitch. I said that what is seen by the naked eye is not what creates and sustains or causes a business or organisation to flourish, stall or flounder. Rather, it is the un*seen* that is the creator, 'sustainer' or destroyer. At a point well into that challenging conversation, my mind, by that point taxed to overload, suddenly cleared. Into that space – The Realm of Possibility – popped the model that follows, which I call 'The Fourth Element of Business and Organisation'.

It was the representation I needed to describe to my now long-time friend what was at cause in the genesis, growth, sustainability, demise and death of any and all businesses and organisations, for profit or not-for-profit (as well as all governments, of whatever persuasion) – and every imaginable aspect of them. This Fourth Element was the genesis of what was at cause in the greater good businesses and other organisations can contribute to society, as well as the harm and destruction they can equally create.

What follows is a fleshed-out version of what I put to my friend.

AN (OLD) NEW PARADIGM

The quality of our collective thinking alone determines the success, mediocrity or failure of our businesses or organisation and, more critically, whether they serve the common good.

Many claim authorship of a new paradigm, a model so revolutionary that it literally shifts our understanding of and response to the world in which we live and work. I make no such claim because this model, though unrecognised by most, unnamed till now and mostly unexplained in the context of business and organisation, has existed all along. It is as ancient as time, and as new as your next brilliant idea. Yet it's as revolutionary for business and organisations as the understanding of gravity is for aeronautical and structural engineering.

This understanding promises – no, it guarantees – a transformation (not linear change) of the way businesses and organisations are created and operated, and consequently their contribution to the betterment of the individuals involved, their suppliers and clients, the community they serve and the world at large.

Will this guide be a catalyst for the renaissance of business and organisations seeing the light of day? That is my vision. You decide if you think I'm away with the fairies!

What follows (and what this book is saying from the first to the last word) is at the heart of the viability and sustainability of any business or not-for-profit organisation; and equally, their non-viability and unsustainability. More critically, it's what the corporate world and all governments need to understand to restore the health and sustainability of our collective home, Earth.

Corporations (for-profit and not-for-profit) and governments at all levels are in urgent need of a new paradigm. They are presently stuck in one that seems self-serving (bordering on self-destructive) rather than in service to humanity and the common good.

Because the first three elements of business and organisation – skills, systems and finances – receive pretty much 100 per cent of management's focus and resources, culture – the product of Thought – is neglected or, worse, disregarded.

I repeat, for ease of explanation, I have grouped the various aspects of business and organisation under three broad headings to deal with the increasing complexity of the world of business and the organisation. As there is much overlap between elements one, two and three, I leave myself open to being dismissed as not understanding this world. I trust my seven decades spent in, and my intimacy with that world, from a young child till today, will alleviate any such concerns.

These three elements are highly developed, analysed, understood and documented. Each is essential to the set-up, growth and sustainability of any business or organisation. These three are the nuts and bolts of all institutions (private, community and state) and are tangible and recognisable to each of us, whether we are familiar with business, organisation and government or not.

But then there's the Fourth Element: Thought.

At present, its DNA, its all-encompassing role in corporations (large and small – for-profit or not-for-profit – private, public or government) is little recognised, unfamiliar to most and intangible to everyone except those that *see* its omnipotence. Yet Element Four is both the genesis of every business or organisation and the meta-element that creates, formulates and feeds the other three and any and every aspect of them.

- Thought is at cause and works the controls in every nook and cranny of every business or organisation.
- It is the source of every aspect of their beginnings, evolution and unravelling.
- It is the birthplace of success, mediocrity or failure.
- It is the genesis of Possibility and impossibility.

Thought and its product, our thinking, alone determine how practical, productive and beneficial or otherwise the skills, systems and finances are. There is nothing but Thought at work each nanosecond of every 24 hours.

Consider please whether this perspective provides the ultimate vantage point from which to look at and understand yourself, your colleagues, your business or organisation.

The law of gravity was laced with controversy and disputed conceptual ownership from inception through to an acceptance that it is *what is*. Gravity was intangible, nebulous, and complex. Its discovery was also the paradigm shift of its time.

The Fourth Element of Business and Organisation is also without voice and hidden from sight, but will eventually emerge, not equal to but *primary* to the way we look at, understand and go about doing business, operating organisations and governments.

BEING HALF AWAKE

> *Waking up is seeing <u>that</u> we think, that <u>what</u> we think is our reality, and that our reality is either created within our mind from seeing life through the lens of our past, and thus impossibility; or seeing what is and endless Possibility.*

To create context, let's overview briefly the first three elements, the ones we currently embrace as being the current, daily reality for business and organisation. These are the three tangibles we in businesses and organisations now expend most if not all our money, time, training and energy on.

We forget, or don't *see* (and, as a consequence, are ignorant of) the primary cause-and-effect relationship between the Fourth Element and the other three elements. In this, the overwhelming majority of us leaders of businesses and organisations are half awake.

We see and implement these three tangible elements as our priorities; however, as a consequence, we lead ultimately 'us too' organisations doing the limited best we can see to do. We don't recognise and therefore don't understand the genesis of success, mediocrity and failure and, at the level of cause and effect, what it takes to optimise the value of these three elements.

The primary force at work – in reality, the *only* force at work, and the one that strategic plans and mission statements and internal policies and procedures neglect or make only obscure reference to – is left unharnessed. Little wonder then that businesses and organisations experience so much trouble surviving (let alone thriving), and have difficulty fusing what their leaders *say* in these documents with what they actually *do* on a day-to-day basis.

Element One: Skills

Skills are the fusing of human ability, training, knowledge and experience, expressed at the many levels of proficiency brought to the business or organisation by its people. Accounting, welding, selling, engineering, writing, medicine, training, sewing, supervising, building, programming and deep-sea diving are all skills.

Skills are the **crafts** we use that, in concert with how awake we are to Element Four, determine the level of effectiveness in designing, producing and delivering our products or services.

Element Two: Systems

Systems are the amalgam of human-created procedures, processes, plans, routines, practices, policies, programs, methods and models used within the business to operate and help manage and maintain it.

Systems are the **concepts** devised for running the business or organisation at optimal efficiency and effectiveness. They are developed and achieve their purpose – again – to the degree we are awake to the Fourth Element and its pivotal role in: a) their creation, b) optimising their use, c) rendering useless all systems, and d) the degrees of utilisation or non-utilisation in between a) and c).

Element Three: Finance

Finance takes many forms: stock, debtors, creditors, borrowings, leased or owned buildings, plant, machinery, equipment, locations, hardware and the entire infrastructure utilised in doing business and operating organisations – including all of Elements One and Two. It is the **capital** employed and deployed to fund the enterprise. And yes, how well deployed or wasted the financial resources of the business or organisation are depends yet again on how awake we are to the Fourth Element.

Within the context of these three broad categories, let's look in more detail at what's foundational to them – the Fourth Element of Business and Organisation: Thought.

ELEMENT FOUR: THOUGHT

Thought is the intangible, invisible but ever-present **context** from which each individual creates their life and performs their various roles for better or worse. It is the originating force behind Elements One, Two and Three, and it alone determines the degree to which each works for or against the organisation and the common good. Thought is the *ground of being* from which the intellectual property is created and the organisation grows and functions well – or self-destructs due to the dysfunctional thinking of its people, and dies from out-dated ideas.

The degree to which Thought is recognised and capitalised on as being the *sole* determinant of everything (good, bad and indifferent) in the business or organisation is a function of the level of awareness, of the collective consciousness, existing within the organisation. Element Four alone is the moment-to-moment working reality of the enterprise, and it alone governs how the affairs of the business or organisation are conducted. Elements One, Two and Three are all created by and subject to Element Four in each moment and in every aspect of their creation, utilisation, decline or reformation. Element Four is the creative, sustaining and destructive force in every organisation.

Yes, I have hammered this to death, but dismiss the message at your peril.

THE LACK OF CONSCIOUSNESS IS ALL THAT AILS CAPITALISM

In a world where hard-headed, no-holds-barred decisions seem mandatory, businesses and organisations might well ask, 'What has Thought and our awareness of it got to do with our very real, very tangible, very pressing imperatives?' (You could well be saying: 'John Wood, what a deluded flake you are.')

In response to the likelihood of that thinking, I offer this reflection: *the state we are in – Possibility or impossibility – indisputably determines the path on which we walk (every one of us) at every level of the organisation: the high road or the low road, a state of Possibility or impossibility. The two paths travelled to ultimate success or failure.*

The quality of our thinking is the *only* factor at work (for better or worse) throughout every organisation on Earth, from charperson to chairperson. Thought *alone* rules – not the market conditions, not our competitors, peers, subordinates, supervisors, board, customers or suppliers. Nor do our bankers, government regulators and their regulations and taxes rule. It is not an outside-in world, and all of these factors are outside our mind, and therefore our control. Our reality is inside-out created. If we understand this, we can be our best selves, our true selves, and be in service to the common good while also being successful.

How we engage, disengage, harness up to or unharness from the world we work in – how we see or *see* that world – alone determines our and our organisations' fate. It's not market forces. How we see or *see* reality is the key determinant.

In a state of impossibility, it seems to us that external factors do determine our success, failure or otherwise – that we are the victims of the ever-shifting circumstances of the market (and of our life).

In another state – one of Possibility – we *see* that it is us, not 'them' or any other external factors that determine our success or failure, happiness or sadness. The 'buck stops' with us. Our thinking, our internal environment – not the external environment, not the economic or the myriad other circumstances we find ourselves in – determines how we handle our job and our organisation, and therefore how creative, efficient and effective we are in each moment, and how we have been in every preceding moment.

Have we *seen* or – right now – are we *seeing* the *what is* of each opportunity and threat? Or, have we seen or are we seeing – right now – only our conditioned imaginings of these?

Those are two primary questions we must have foremost in mind and ask ourselves and each other constantly if we want to stay open to Possibility and lead a truly sustainable organisation.

To recognise the prevailing state/s of consciousness within our organisation (individually and collectively) is to *see* and understand the ultimate meta-influence of Thought and its product – our thinking, feelings and actions, our states of Possibility or impossibility – on our business and organisational environment.

To be awake to these facts of how we each create our human experience is to be at the peak of our human power to influence our organisation in our most creative, constructive and productive way and its contribution to the common good.

But this meta-reality has to be *seen* by us individually for it to have legitimacy in our awareness. Our awakening to and therefore our understanding of Thought and how it, and it alone, is in charge of the organisation enables that legitimacy. Consequently, that consciousness, that state of awareness enables us, one by one, to utilise this core power for – rather than against – the business and organisation, and for – rather than against – our fellow humans, all other sentient beings and the environment.

There is Thought – all that is created is the result of it. But to harness its power, we must first wake up and experience the sweetness of that reality.

How Australia won the America's Cup

The prestigious yacht race, the America's Cup, was first held in 1851. The New York Yacht Club won every staging of the event for the next 132 years – the longest winning streak in history in any sport. Australia first contested the Cup in 1962, and promptly joined the long list of losers.

As the winner got to host the next event, every race was held in the US, usually the Rhode Island area. Australia again had the opportunity to challenge in 1983 – once more in Rhode Island – with currents and winds the American sailors knew oh so well.

As the event drew near, the contesting yachts were displayed for the media. But the hull of *Australia II*, the challenger, was always covered in drapes, hidden from prying eyes and cameras. The whispers began: why all this secrecy? What are they hiding? This subterfuge infuriated the Americans, who called for the yacht to be disqualified. Of course, we all now know what was being hidden, and with good reason: that keel – the legendary, revolutionary 'winged keel' – gave *Australia II* the edge it needed for us to finally wrench that cup from the hands of America. That keel achieved instant immortality – and for the Americans, eternal infamy. So, what was so special about it?

The winglet on each side of the keel increases the aspect ratio of the vessel, which reduces the amount of drag through the water, minimising resistance to the boat's movement. It also increases lift in the water. These advantages work regardless of whether the vessel is sailing into the wind, at an angle to it, or with it.

The other key innovation is that the winged keel inverts the traditional keel, which has its greatest bulk at the top. The winged keel resembles an upside-down champagne glass (not a flute) or an upside-down handheld fan: its greatest mass is lower in the water.

There is some dispute over whose invention the winged keel actually is. Any which way, the point is that someone – Ben Lexcen, Peter van Oossanen, whoever – *saw* something no one had before, made it happen, and was stunningly successful, forever changing the landscape in which they operated.

That's Possibility at work.

OUR UNDERSTANDING OF THOUGHT DETERMINES OUR ACCESS TO POSSIBILITY

Any explanation of this phenomenon will only be useful to the extent that it stirs you and your own *seeing* into The Realm of Possibility.

Thought (in its unformed or energetic state) is the energy, you could say, the Life force enabling us to live and experience life as human beings. This energy is detected by an EEC machine. That process is called electroencephalography. It is this electrophysiological monitoring method that records electrical activity in the brain.

Thought manifesting as a combination of original ideas and useful memorised ones creates and sustains our organisations. Our collective thinking, therefore, manifests each nanosecond throughout every nook and cranny of our businesses and organisations in ways that contribute to success or failure.

Ultimately, *status-quo* thinking can never stop the organisation from sinking into oblivion.

Original Thought (fresh or unique thinking) is the unrecognised and thus under-utilised resource in all that we do. It's under-utilised because we lack the understanding of its value – not only in the area of invention and innovation, but also in the qualities of kindness, understanding, wisdom and common sense inherent in The Realm of Possibility. I can't explain why that is so. I make this claim because that is how it is for me and for growing numbers of people.

At the same time, our creative thinking (original or fresh Thought) is disruptive. Fresh Thought questions, challenges and throws the spotlight on the *status quo* and has us continually assessing the value and relevance of what we are doing, and if found wanting, *seeing* new and improved ways forward.

Impossibility thinking (our memory/conditioning) – if in charge – blocks that original source of renewal.

Fortunately, impossibility thinking can never survive the flow of fresh or original Thought. And so it is up to us to consciously pull the plug on our past (even from a moment ago) to allow that fresh flow of Thought.

As explained elsewhere, although we get fresh ideas, for most of us these ideas relate to what really interests us. A football coach will get a fresh *insight* into how to play the game in a new way, which wins his or her team a premiership. A yacht designer comes up with a revolutionary keel design, which contributes to Australia winning the America's Cup.

Now, if that coach doesn't stay creative in the way he or she strategises and coaches the team, they won't continue to be successful, because just as the winged keel contributed to Australia's success, other fresh ideas, innovations and new strategies created within the minds of the US team won the Cup back from Australia four years later.

That formed state of our thinking (knowledge), as critically important and as necessary as much of it is, remains the realm of impossibility until we actually *see* and therefore understand Thought as the wellspring of our reality (either fresh or recycled) – either Possibility or impossibility.

We can *see* life afresh or we can unconsciously recycle our memories, thereby limited to seeing life through the prism of our past.

Our understanding of the primacy of Thought in our life and our organisations is the degree to which we *see* with clarity the cause and effect of all we think on – our feelings and actions and the world we are creating in each moment. The degree to which we *see* our own and everyone else's thinking as the determinant of every aspect of business and organisation determines how successfully we can recognise Possibility and impossibility in our self and in others.

How?

Failing to understand that Thought and its product, our thinking, our feelings and our actions, have ultimate control over the business or organisation constricts the organisation's potential, at best; or destroys it, at worst.

Whatever thinking we are experiencing in each moment reflects the way we are *seeing* or failing to see how we are creating our reality, our life, our business or organisation, our world.

Our thinking reflects the extent to which we are awake or asleep as human beings, as conscious or unconscious individuals.

WHAT IS MISSING IN OUR UNDERSTANDING?

Thought's manifestations – concepts such as attitude, creativity, determination, adaptability, persistence, love, gratitude, etc. and their opposites – are seen as important, but are considered and explored as if they exist without a single, primary cause.

However, the *source* of those qualities and our entire noble and ignoble personal attributes, Thought, is barely understood and therefore hardly recognised, at least within the world of business and organisations. How Thought manifests in and through us is yet to be *seen* as the basis of success and failure – of sustainability and unsustainability.

Consequently, to date, few leaders have capitalised on the unlimited potential that this understanding holds for their organisation and the common good of humanity. Whether we *see* it or not, Thought plays out in the workplace and the world through the lives of each of us, every nanosecond of every day, as either life-affirming or life-denying.

Allan Helps William *See*

Seeing our conditioned thinking for the slippery customer it is, is our number-one challenge and our most precious reward.

Many years ago, a powerful example of how we get trapped in the maze of our thinking was brought home to me when a colleague related a story about a senior and critically important member of a large law firm.

Allan had been called in by the firm's managing partner to assist in resolving difficulties with a partner, William, who was a gifted and brilliant lawyer in a highly specialised area of corporate law. He was recognised nationally as the pre-eminent person in his field. The problem was that William had increasingly dire relations with other partners whom he regularly came in contact with. Their support staff also dreaded contact with him. Morale around him was rock-bottom, and the turnover rate of his immediate subordinates was unsustainably high.

To compound the difficulties, which seemingly were beyond salvaging by the time Allan became involved, the firm's largest fee-paying client (linked in business to several other clients they had introduced to the firm) saw itself as dependent on the extraordinary quality of William's work, as did some other clients.

So William's leaving would create a cascading loss of clients, revenue and staff. Everyone in the law firm conceded that William's work was nothing short of remarkable. Sacking him was a frightening option. Having more partners leave (two already had), along with some of their staff and clients, would be equally devastating to the firm. And newcomers were even less likely to tolerate William's increasingly dysfunctional behaviour. It was a bizarre situation.

William reluctantly agreed to meet with Allan out of deference to Megan, the HR Director. She was new to the firm and one of the few with whom William still managed to have semi-civil relations. And in the light of the personal inconveniences he was experiencing with the rapid-fire attrition of his staff, his back was to the wall. Megan was familiar with Allan's work; she had participated in some programs with him on Possibility some years before, and she reckoned that only someone with Allan's understanding of how people in distress function had any chance of reaching William and being a catalyst for transforming the unmitigated mess in which the company found itself.

From William's perspective, the problems were clear-cut. They were a direct result of everyone else's incompetence bordering on stupidity. In William's first meeting with Allan, he challenged Allan's competence and made it blatantly clear that he strongly doubted Allan would bring any value. This came as no surprise to Allan. William asked things like, 'What size law firms have you worked with?' And more specifically, 'How many partners, associates and support staff did those firms have?' He also asked, 'What type of law did they practise and what type of clients did they work with?'

William believed that, unless there was a very close match, Allan would not be capable of working with him or the firm. As it was, Allan had not worked with a law firm remotely like the one William worked for. When Allan put forward an accounting practice he had worked with that had roughly the same structure, numbers and clients with similar profiles, William was adamant that there were no parallels between law and accounting firms. They were, according to William, chalk and cheese. He believed you could not generalise about companies, their people and their circumstances. Experience, in his reality, wasn't portable and couldn't be generalised.

He is an excellent example of how our memory of the past obscures our thinking in the present. For William, the specific technical knowledge one learns is the only knowledge of value. He couldn't *see what is*. He saw only his conditioned reality. As the saying goes, there are none so blind as those who will not *see*.

But with gentle coaching, Possibility reveals itself to most people, if not all. Bit by bit, over some months, Allan established a rapport with William, helped him calm down, and supported him in finding his way through the density of his thinking (using Vertical inquiry – see Chapter 6).

Allan wasn't thrown by William's brilliant mind and boxed-in thinking. Neither was he reactive against it. With this neutrality, coupled with his kindness, understanding, wisdom and common sense, he was able to point a way forward. Or rather, Possibility revealed itself to William, as it always will if given a chance. With a calming mind, William started to experience some critical *insights*. He began to recognise his beliefs, opinions and judgements, and *saw* how these were driving his feelings and behaviour.

Those around William got help as well. Conditions improved, especially when Allan began working with William's peers and the support staff around Thought, Possibility and impossibility. They experienced a new level of understanding between them all, and Possibility was *seen* by several individuals within the group. This new understanding laid the foundation for a lasting solution.

We're all a bit like William. If you imagine you are different or special, you do not *see what is*. When experiencing life in the restricted way William did (and we all do, to varying degrees), we're dead certain that the circumstances of our life determine the way we see and experience the world. We don't *see* that Thought in each new moment enables our very existence and it alone determines whether we live from Possibility or impossibility. But just as it was for him, it's difficult for each of us to *see* our own entrenched views, as well as our reactivity to circumstances, and commitment to the personal reality we know and experience to be 'the truth'.

William was, as Megan suspected, diagnosed with a mild form of Asperger's Syndrome that had become extremely problematic as his client load increased and he had become increasingly busy-minded, stressed, anxious and obsessive. This diagnosis threw fresh light on the challenges he faced and those his colleagues faced in relating and working with him in a responsive rather than reactive way.

I have been intrigued over the years to find this deeply ingrained thinking (minus the added weight of Asperger's Syndrome) to be common in groups and individuals I have worked with. Rigid conditioned thinking – even extremely disordered thinking, as in William's case – places others and us in boxes that are difficult to *see* into or out of. Yet Possibility is available to everyone even in the direst situations (unless brain-damaged beyond normal functioning).

When we're stuck in our beliefs, we imagine that only others just like us can relate to our problems, challenges and ways of looking at life. 'Just like us' includes factors as diverse as upbringing, specific training and employment status, the type and size of the organisation, political inclinations, religion and more. It's difficult for us, given our life-long conditioning, to recognise that fundamentally we are all the same – each a product of what is going on in our mind.

Seeing or not seeing that we create our reality moment by moment via our thinking is all that separates us from peace and harmony – or upset and frustration. *Seeing* that we think enables us to live in a state of kindness, understanding, wisdom and common sense. Failing to *see* precludes us from doing so.

At this moment, you may be having an increasingly strong reaction to what I have been saying. You might feel like telling me a thing or two, or consigning this guide to the bin. You may be sick and tired of hearing me talk about intangibles.

You might be thinking:

- John doesn't understand my business or circumstances.
- He's not under the financial pressures that I'm under.
- All these fancy concepts are nice, but I've got a bottom line to manage – and very demanding shareholders.
- The world of business, government, organisations, etc. is different now. What would he know that is relevant in today's world?
- 'I have read better, different, more relevant books, guides and writings on what makes an organisation tick.'

If any of this relates to you, as it does to me, we are simply being human. Our reactions at such times come from our un*seen*, unrecognised certainties: invisible beliefs that we are certain are 'the truth of the matter'. And, as such, we don't like them violated. Our emotional reactivity (a sure sign we are in impossibility) when a new idea clashes with our pre-existing worldview can be intense. We feel uncomfortable, at sea, sometimes enraged. We resist and make the new idea wrong. We have a need for certainty – the certainty of our 'truth'.

Though it can be shattering, it's always liberating when, after investing a lifetime holding certain beliefs, we *see* them from a higher vantage point – a place of greater awareness. It's not a matter of throwing out beliefs. We can't while we still believe them. What happens to a belief we've *seen* through is that it abandons us.

HOW THE THREE OTHER ELEMENTS ARE CREATED BY THOUGHT

Here are some examples of the cause and effect of Thought on the other three elements.

ELEMENT ONE: SKILLS

If we haven't yet *seen* that we habitually create our reality via our conditioning, i.e. our impossibility thinking, our performance may reflect high skill, like William, but overriding that will be our counterproductive thinking and therefore our unhelpful attitudes and behaviour. However highly skilled we may be, as William was, if we are dominated by our past – our knowledge, beliefs, opinions and judgements – and especially if they are less than helpful, we are stuck with an equally-less-than-helpful mindset.

For example, we may be judgemental and critical of subordinates, threatened and intimidated by peers, or obsequious and submissive with supervisors. Or a mixture of these.

On the other hand, experiencing life from Possibility and consequently released from our habitual insecure thinking, we *see* our co-workers in a new light of goodwill and cooperation. Our contribution to our fellow travellers is exponentially more helpful and our life more enjoyable. We are free to relate as equals – neither superior nor inferior.

Even if we possess only average skill but are not imprisoned by negative beliefs, opinions and judgements, we are at peace with, open to and supportive of others. We live mostly from that healthier state of awareness. Free to *see* Possibility to whatever degree we do, our contribution to our organisation is, on balance, beyond our skill level.

We respond well to training, are open to Possibility in all its manifestations, and are a pleasure to work with. We are helpful, kind and decent. We enjoy our work and life in general and are sought-after as an employee, as a friend and as a boss. In short, our attitude (a direct reflection of our level of self-awareness of Thought) amplifies our contribution to our organisation in either a constructive or destructive way, regardless of our skill level. You may question that, as is sensible to do. But no matter how skilful and vital to the organisation William was, as you have read, until he realised his negative impact, he was tearing the practice apart.

ELEMENT TWO: SYSTEMS

Businesses and organisations want to stay on or, better still, ahead of the curve, so they introduce systems intended to work more efficiently and effectively. Often these attempts fail. Why?

There are many reasons attributed to this failure, but there's actually only one: impossibility thinking. If people's thinking sabotages any stage – i.e. the search for, acquisition of, introduction and/or use of these systems – the organisation will not derive the benefits a better system should provide.

And, in a free-market environment, organisations need to improve – or go backwards.

If we're one of these saboteurs, we can and do frustrate the sourcing, implementation and use of new systems. We may even be in a position of sufficient influence to block the idea from getting to the exploration stage.

And then there's the belief that a new, better or more sophisticated system will fix the problems created by poor attitudes. That won't work either, and it will waste money and other resources. These problems will not be front-page news to anyone that has worked in a business, government or not-for-profit organisation.

Conversely, an organisation with outdated or inadequate systems, but whose people happily make the most of what they have and work the system to its optimal potential, will stay competitive and in service. These are the people that make up, to the extent possible, for deficiencies in an outmoded, inefficient system or technology by their willingness to make the most of what they have.

Any system is neutral in and of itself. It is what we humans do or don't do with it that has it contributing to or subtracting from the smooth running, increased productivity, success and sustainability of the organisation.

ELEMENT THREE: FINANCE

Again, it isn't uncommon to see a large organisation with the most modern plant and equipment, beautiful buildings, and more capital resources than they need, outperformed by a smaller, under-resourced one with a more creative, dynamic and happy workforce. Outperformed, that is, by Possibility-*seers* who respond to their customers, to the marketplace and to each other. Look at how IBM, a Goliath in pre-Internet days, was left behind and cut out of certain markets by sleeker, smarter computer-based companies like Apple and Microsoft as the world began embracing cyberspace. All their expertise, their resources, their reputation, their global reach couldn't keep IBM dominating the computer world, because the world had changed and they couldn't change fast enough with it. These Possibility-*seers*, often referred to as 'can-do people' are more likely to *see what is*, rather than viewing circumstances through their beliefs, opinions and judgements, restricted by their existing knowledge.

Lack of finance didn't affect the thinking that created the platform for PCs. That discovery was born in a garage. The amazingly successful Microsoft was the result. And what a contribution to the common good the organisation has made and continues to make to this day. Even its detractors concede that point.

IN SUMMARY

The realm of Possibility is the antithesis of all our certainty about how things are or should be.

The clarity with which the board of directors, CEO, the senior leadership group and each member of the organisation recognise the all-encompassing role of Thought in the life, vitality, success and failure of the organisation determines the extent to which the business or organisation is delivering the promise (see 'Being in service is "delivering the Promise"' in Chapter 5).

Thought rules supreme. Each individual, you or me, and the collective states of mind (the weight of numbers either experiencing Possibility or impossibility thinking) within the organisation determine:

- the organisation's capacity to create, innovate, implement and sustain;
- whether there are sufficient numbers who *see* and understand the outcomes sought to deliver the promise implicit in the organisation being in existence;
- whether sufficient individuals have personal and organisational outcomes in mind that are in synergy;

- the quality and effectiveness of internal and external communications;
- the quality and effectiveness of teamwork;
- the climate of commitment and goodwill towards all stakeholders;
- whether conflicts are created and, if they are, how they are resolved;
- the degree to which colleagues let go of the past and open up to fresh ways of working and interacting with each other and with other stakeholders;
- how members fore*see* and respond to market conditions;
- whether the organisation contributes to the common good or subtracts from it;
- the bottom line – success or failure, profit or loss. Thrive or wither.

CHAPTER 4

CASE STUDY: IMPLEMENTING POSSIBILITY IN AN ORGANISATION

'Create a great culture, and you create a great company.'

I wrote the following letter to my son, John, back in the early 2000s when he, as the founder and CEO of National Lifestyle Villages (NLV), was considering options around turning their villages into sustainable communities.

It provides a model and a process for creating and maintaining a high-functioning and therefore sustainable community of people.

It outlines an approach to:

- Preventing the residents (called 'lifestylers' by the company) and company personnel in John's villages from forming a 'them and us' dichotomy with the resultant difficulties and downsides that creates.

- Limiting the inevitable formation of cliques, factions, elites and in-groups in the village community which are counterproductive to the sustainability of, in this case, the lifestyle village as a psychologically healthy, integrated community where the needs of all are responded to with impartiality.

The model outlined is suitable and adaptable for businesses or organisations, such as a company board, an executive group, creative group, any workgroup within the private, government or NGO sectors. Any group of people wanting to perform at their cohesive best would be suited to the process recommended. (I suggest that the application of the model would be equally effective for any group of people looking for kindness, understanding, wisdom and common sense in their relationships.)

Any person with the required skills and heart-felt inclinations could introduce and facilitate the process (adapted to suit the specific needs of the context), thereby fostering the concept of living and working from Possibility rather than impossibility for their company or organisation.

It is an outline that any aware leader, inspired by the potential of living from Possibility, could explore when considering transforming their organisation into a unified, cross-pollinating, innovative and sustainable community that individually and collectively *sees* Possibility.

For the ideas in this outline to materialise and bear fruit, much open discussion, deep listening, tweaking and some trialling would need to take place. And for all of that to be successful, it is to be facilitated and influenced from The Realm of Possibility.

Note: John sold his company in 2018.

INTRODUCTION

'Hell, there are no rules here, we are trying to accomplish something.'

Thomas Edison

The company, NLV, creates residential communities dispersed over an ever-expanding geographical area in WA. They aim to provide sustainable communities that are affordable, safe, fun and provide an enriching and healthy lifestyle for active over-45-year-olds.

Creating a sustainable community is an age-old pursuit. All groups of people of all ages, including families and people of like mind, face the challenges of living and working together harmoniously (and thus sustainably).

It seems to make little difference what community we talk about, as the challenges faced are common to all. Whether the group is a common-interest group, a sporting body, trade association, NGO, private business, workers' union, government agency, or public corporation, lifestyle village, commune or kibbutz, the challenges in creating and sustaining a healthy, happy community are as one.

The human-relations issues all groups face, large or small, are universal. The challenge is in knowing what it takes to grow and maintain sustainable relationships – the essence of a sustainable community. How your village lifestylers might create closer and more lasting relationships (while remaining non-intrusive) can be distilled into a handful of key elements.

These, if genuinely and thoughtfully addressed within each community, create the context for long-term harmony and satisfaction in each village. What makes that possible is a yearning for peaceful community that already exists within the minds and hearts of all of us however hidden it may be. Village lifestylers are no exception; instead, the fact that they live in such an environment *is a testimony to their desire for community*.

If the village life-stylers do not experience the key elements outlined below, disharmony will occur. Their lack will make life much less pleasant for lifestylers and more difficult for NLV management in delivering their promise of providing an *enriching lifestyle*. If not in place, these key elements will inevitably lead to:

- A reduced return for shareholders, as the NLV concept will not realise its potential to enrich the environment and thus the lives of their lifestylers.

- The cost-free word-of-mouth endorsements to potential new lifestylers of NLV will not be as high in number or as rich in passion.

- The implicit promise of NLV will not be delivered to the various stakeholders involved – life-stylers, their families, staff, investors, the industry as a whole, the broader community, and governments looking for alternative sustainable and affordable community housing options.

The key elements referred to above would resonate with most village lifestylers as:

- The feeling of being an integral and authentically valued member of the village community rather than a commercial commodity.

- An experience of being seen, heard and considered by others (company staff and other life-stylers) within the village.

- Knowing in one's heart that kindness, understanding, wisdom and common sense are core values embraced, fostered and lived by NLV team members and fellow lifestylers.

Sustainable design stems from the union of **'doing what works'** with **'doing what matters'** (exactly what this means is explained below). When this union originates from The Realm of Possibility – the meta-context for creating *what really works and what really matters* – amazing things happen to individuals and their relationships.

OVERVIEW

NLV has grown from one village to many, and the organisation faces the challenges inherent in moving from essentially a one-person leadership structure to an organisation with many distinct leaders.

Equally, these leaders need to sustain good relationships with each other, with their suppliers of goods and services and, most critically, with the growing resident/client population. As necessary, but not as apparent, the resident population needs to sustain positive relationships with each other, with NLV personnel and, if the organisation is to capitalise on the sustainable lifestyle created in one village, to also create it in the other villages.

For the NLV community to be sustained at an optimal psychological level, *all stakeholders in NLV* need to understand what you are endeavouring to achieve beyond simply earning a sustainable return on investment, i.e. to add to the richness of the lifestylers' experience.

More than ever, the 21st-century organisation must be based on sustainable principles to survive and prosper into the increasingly uncertain economic future. To achieve that, businesses need to understand more completely what sustainability means. And there is more to that than appears obvious. In this context, apart from being economically viable, it means being capable of staying healthy in relationship, without exhausting each other's or the planet's resources, depleting each other's energy, or damaging other stakeholders in any way. Being sustainable in this deeper sense of the word is key to maintaining the NLV brand and its social licence.

PART ONE: THE CONTEXT NECESSARY FOR CREATING SUSTAINABLE COMMUNITY – NLV'S BOARD AND TEAM

The following will, I trust, create a context for examining the relevance of what I'm proposing. It introduces the concepts underpinning the 'Four Elements of Business and Organisation'.

It appears that NLV (like any business or organisation) is sustained by the *skills, systems and finance* it utilises. These three elements are essential to the proper functioning of all internal and external activities of any business.

Looking deeper, we *see* that these elements are either created and sustained or underutilised, sabotaged or even destroyed by a fourth, all-powerful meta-element: *Thought*. I name these four elements to create a conceptual framework for understanding the workings of the human mind in a business and organisational context.

Thought is the source of all human functioning and activity – the good, the bad and the indifferent. Thought is the power in our mind where the spark of creative genius, innovative capacity, inherent decency and depth of understanding resides. I refer to that facet of Thought as 'Possibility'.

Thought is equally the source and power behind our accumulated knowledge, opinions, judgments, fears and insecurities – the totality of our beliefs – and of our family and cultural conditioning. This accumulation is stored in memory – our conscious and unconscious memory. I refer to that facet of Thought (the form our thinking has taken) as the realm of 'impossibility'.

'DOING WHAT WORKS' AND 'DOING WHAT MATTERS' WITHIN ORGANISATIONS

> *'If we don't understand how we create our culture, our culture will reflect that lack of understanding.'*

Two of the many ways Thought is at work each nanosecond in NLV are when people are considering **what they think works** and/or **what they think matters**. That is, utilising Element Four, they work with elements one, two and three, and their thinking informs them that **this works** or **this doesn't work; this matters** or **this doesn't matter**.

To illustrate the concepts of **'doing what works'** or **'doing what matters'**, consider the two lists below. And note that every point in each list, depending on your perspective, might readily be moved to the other list. As the saying goes: 'One man's meat is another man's poison!'

Doing what we think works in businesses (this list is indicative only):

1. Keeping the capital requirements and the borrowings of the business within sustainable limits. For very good reason, there are 'rules of thumb' that have evolved over many years that need to be factored in.

2. Making certain that the income generated exceeds the expenditure required to sustain the business.
3. Optimising profit to achieve a sustainable return on investment.
4. Minimising costs to ensure competitiveness.
5. Maintaining wages and conditions within the capacity of the business and the market at supportable levels.
6. Minimising wastage.
7. Simultaneously, investing in staff training and their personal development, and keeping it to sustainable levels.
8. Being highly competitive by working tougher, smarter and more creatively.
9. Buying the best-quality stock, materials and services at the lowest prices available.
10. Optimising the selling price of the goods or services provided so they meet both what the market will pay and the level of profit required by the business to be sustainable.
11. Driving the growth and development of the organisation to 1) recognise and meet what the market demands now, and in the future, 2) innovate to expand the market, 3) do that within the absorption rate of the marketplace, and 4) increase the organisation's capacity to meet that growing market.
12. Ensuring a strong and clearly understood management structure and style is in place, utilising high skills, sound systems and sufficient capital.

Doing what we think matters in business:

1. **Being creative and innovative** – coming up with leading-edge ideas, new projects and fresh ways of operating.
2. **High-quality customer service and retention** – 'delivering the promise' to the client.
3. **Taking care of all stakeholders, not just the shareholders** – caring for the environment and the broader community.

4. **High-quality working relationships** – people relating to each other as friends, colleagues, and co-workers. Supporting each other in getting the job done and achieving the outcomes of the organisation.

5. **Workplace leadership** – how the immediate supervisor, team leader, manager or co-ordinator presents him or herself. Their focus is on leadership and organisational energy, not management and administration.

6. **Having a say** – decisions that affect the day-to-day and future of the business and the workplace.

7. **Clear values** – the extent to which people can see and understand the overall purpose and individual behaviours expected in the workplace.

8. **Being safe** – high levels of personal safety, both physical and psychological. Emotional stability and a feeling of being protected, not exploited, by the system.

9. **The built environment** – a high standard of accommodation and fit-out, with regard to the particular industry type.

10. **Recruitment** – getting the right-minded people is important. They need to share the same values and approach to work as the rest of the group.

11. **Pay and conditions** – a place in which the level of income and the basic physical working conditions (hours, access, travel and the like) are met to a reasonable standard, at least to a level that the people who work there see as reasonable.

12. **Learning** – being able to learn on the job, acquire skills and knowledge from everywhere, and develop a greater understanding of the whole workplace.

13. **Passion** – the energy and commitment to the workplace, high levels of volunteering, excitement and a sense of wellbeing. Actually wanting to come to work.

14. **Having fun** – a psychologically secure workplace in which people can relax with each other and enjoy social interaction.

15. **Community connections** – being part of the local community, feeling as though the workplace is a valuable element of local affairs.

16. **Getting feedback** – knowing what people think of each other, their contribution to the success of the place, and their individual performance over time.

17. **Autonomy and uniqueness** – the capacity of the organisation to tolerate and encourage the individual sense of difference that excellent workplaces develop. Their sense of being the best at what they do.

18. **A sense of ownership and identity** – pride in the place of work, knowing the business and controlling the technology.

(Note: this list, except for points 1–3 and with minor modification, is drawn from research entitled 'Simply the Best', UNSW, 2003.)

Again, the above list is not definitive, but is indicative of what matters to people working in organisations.

Let's now look at the needs and values of the various leaders in NLV who, like all human beings, are primarily motivated by either 'doing what they think works' or 'doing what they think matters' – the invisible meta-context that drives the organisation.

THE TWO LEADERSHIP TYPES DRIVEN BY 'DOING WHAT WORKS'

Although a shift is occurring within the world of business and organisations towards 'doing more of what matters', the emphasis on 'doing what works' remains the primary focus of the majority of leaders, particularly in business.

The proponents of 'doing what works' are those that see the function of **production** and **administration** as having unmatched importance in the success of a business. They hold this view almost exclusively when under pressure, to the exclusion of 'doing what matters'. The archetypal **Producer** is all about doing, achieving and output. The archetypal **Administrator** is obsessed with i-dotting, t-crossing, getting it right and keeping it tight.

The heavy conditioning (i.e. the overriding belief system) of the Producer and Administrator means they clash with proponents of 'doing what matters'. The extreme versions of the Producer and Administrator are both ruthlessly hard-nosed and think doing what matters doesn't work, wastes time, has no place in business or organisation, and ought to be confined to one's private life – if that! They argue that the only things that matter are tight control, pushing output to the max, and making a profit at all costs.

This extremely narrow perspective assumes that the sole purpose of business is exercising power and control to maximise profit. It doesn't *see* that profit, particularly profitability sustained over a long period, needs other inputs. It fails to recognise that 'doing what matters' is equally crucial to continuing success and sustainability.

THE TWO LEADERSHIP TYPES DRIVEN BY 'DOING WHAT MATTERS'

While numbers are growing, there is still considerably less support for 'doing what matters' within most commercial organisations (and within government and not-for-profits). Referred to sometimes as 'conscious leadership', the intended result is 'conscious capitalism'.

Two types that fall into the worldview of doing what matters are the **Entrepreneur** and the **Integrator**. With their commonly held predisposition towards 'doing what they think matters', they can easily upset the outcome-oriented, task-directed, more structured worlds of the Producer and Administrator.

Neither the Entrepreneur nor the Integrator seems to grasp that for sound, sustainable profits, high production and sound administration must be kept firmly in mind when making decisions. Neither the Entrepreneur nor Integrator, by personality type, views balancing budgets as a priority as they passionately go about expending resources on 'what they think matters' – including many of the things outlined in the second list above.

The archetypal Entrepreneur, with his often loose, unpredictable and creative ways, even drives the Integrator to desperation with the constant state of change he (quite unconsciously) inflicts on the organisation, an unstable state in which, of the four leadership types, he alone is comfortable.

By comparison, the Integrator's overarching concern is to ensure the workers don't become cannon fodder in achieving the ever-changing big-picture and organisational direction envisioned by the Entrepreneur, the pressure-cooker environment created by the Producer, or the red tape and nit-picking world of the archetypal Administrator. The archetypal Integrator is genuinely concerned about people's welfare, and the extreme version will gather staff together, link arms and sing 'Kumbaya' as the liquidator walks in to wrap the organisation up.

So we have four different personalities: two who primarily 'do what they think works' and two who mainly 'do what they think matters'. I suspect you will recognise the Producer, Administrator, Entrepreneur and Integrator types in NLV and other organisations you are familiar with; maybe even in yourself. While we all have some of each, most of us are strong in one and weaker in the others.

THE INHERENT CHALLENGES BETWEEN THE FOUR TYPES

The naturally occurring tensions created by these four differing worldviews can, unless understood and respected, affect the relationships between these four types when they don't understand, value and embrace the separate reality in which each of them lives and works.

The Entrepreneur and Integrator tend to be 'loose around the joints', valuing process and the day-to-day joy and thrill of the human journey rather than the nose-to-the-grindstone approach of the Producer and Administrator. The latter two tend to be 'very tight around the joints', outcome-oriented with day-to-day discipline, procedures, protocols, achievement, meeting targets, etc. high on their list.

The more extreme versions of the Entrepreneur and Integrator are often seen as being 'away with the fairies'. What these two think 'matters' is often considered a waste of time and money down the drain by the Producer and Administrator.

The equivalent versions of the Producer and Administrator are often seen as being 'uptight, driven and rigid'. What these two think 'works' is considered counterproductive by the Entrepreneur and Integrator and a block to the organisation's proper functioning.

The puzzle is that the Producer and Administrator equally think 'what we do matters', and the Entrepreneur and Integrator think 'what we do works best!' The fact is that, without the contribution of all four in an integrated way, mismanagement occurs, sustainability is undermined, and the organisation flounders.

A FIFTH TYPE

In every moribund (failing/waning/seen-better-days) business or organisational environment, a fifth type, **Dead Wood**, has assumed significant influence or even control of the enterprise. This type has become disillusioned, disaffected and cynical. Self-survival is of paramount importance. Dead Wood is not motivated to produce, is slack in administration, devoid of entrepreneurial spark and gives little heed to the social integration of others. Dead Wood is alive physically but psychologically dead.

Note: This schema of these five types is adapted from the work of Ichak Adizes, *How to Solve the Mismanagement Crisis: Diagnosis and Treatment of Management Problems*.)

DO THESE FIVE TYPES SHAPE BUSINESSES, OR IS A META-CONTEXT PULLING THE STRINGS?

In considering which management types are shaping NLV, three questions arise:

1. If the disharmony created by the thinking of the five influential personalities is at the root of leadership mismanagement and of indirectly causing a high percentage of businesses or organisations to flounder or fail, why can't the four essential types get their acts together for the sake of business harmony, success and organisational sustainability? Or, you could say, for the common good.

2. In those businesses and organisations that don't fail, why do so many still become dysfunctional and horrid places to work in or do business with?

3. Moreover, why, even in businesses going quite well, is it so hard to get cooperation, people 'delivering the promise' of the organisation and maintaining the ongoing creativity, innovation and renewal?

POSSIBILITY (ORIGINAL THOUGHT) CREATES THE CONTEXT FOR SUSTAINABLE LEADERSHIP

The union of doing what works with what matters really does work and really does matter when experienced within a context of kindness, understanding, wisdom and common sense – The Realm of fresh Thought and Possibility.

High-quality, sustainable relationships are created, and organisational outcomes achieved and sustained when there is a convergence of 'doing what works and what matters'. As they are at the heart of creating the context necessary for sustained success, I define the four non-business terms just used:

- **Kindness** is the feeling of, and expression of warmth, unconditional respect, goodwill and regard for all others. For example – love or kindness is our instinct when we *see* beyond our need to be right and to make others wrong.

- **Understanding** is our innate (and mostly under-utilised) capacity to explore any subject, question or dispute free of our opinion, belief and judgement, not bound by our specific knowledge or expertise. We are present to another's worldview, free of the need to correct or change them.

- **Wisdom** is the capacity to act from a coalescing of *insight*, perceptiveness, clarity and discernment.

- **Common sense** (like wisdom) is a coalescing of our inherent natural intelligence, accumulated knowledge and experience of life in general. It is honed within The Realm of Possibility.

Operated in a context of kindness, understanding, wisdom and common sense, the business maintains:

1. its creativity/entrepreneurship;
2. its people focus/integration;
3. high output/productivity;
4. sound bureaucracy/administration.

These four elements are essential for growing a sustainable organisation. Such an organisation, operating in the cultural environment of Possibility, won't fall prey to the fifth element – Dead-Wood leadership – but instead will continue to move to a new level of operating. We have achieved the degree of conscious leadership, the state of awareness necessary for Possibility to be *seen* ever more clearly.

Without a context of Possibility existing within the minds of the leadership, the organisation is not sustainable over the medium to long-term and will ultimately fail or be taken over. (See the section 'Of Two States of Minds – Conscious and Unconscious Leadership'.)

Conscious leadership results from us becoming self-aware – waking up to how we create our moment-to-moment reality, to the fact that we think into existence the reality we are seeing or *seeing*. In that awakening, we recognise our primary type and what we bring to the table. We also recognise others' primary types, and we respect what they bring to the organisation and their critical importance to its sustainability.

In becoming more conscious, we also become aware of others' thinking and the danger inherent in taking our thinking as being 'the truth'. We *see* that, when we do, we shut down to Possibility. Our understanding will continue to deepen, provided we keep looking further within that state of unsullied awareness. And provided we hold our intention, our *insights* will lead us inevitably to a deeper level of self-awareness and into a realm of understanding that brings forth an experience of kindness towards ourselves and others.

The wisdom and common sense integral to that state guide us to live sustainably in all aspects of life. Newly envisioned and cleansed, we *see what is* rather than seeing a reality reflecting our imaginings. We increasingly *see* and experience life from the context of *'what really works'* and *'what really matters'*. We *see* life beyond our conditioning and into The Realm of Possibility.

THE VANTAGE POINT OF THE CONSCIOUS LEADER

Let's consider the two lists above – 'Doing What Works' and 'Doing What Matters' – from the state of awareness in which we *see* **what really works and what really matters**, the realm of conscious leadership and Possibility. Point two from the 'What Works' list states: *Making certain that the income generated exceeds the expenditure required to sustain the business.* Point three from that list states: *Optimising profit to achieve a sustainable return on investment.*

For a conscious leader, it is still crystal clear that *income must exceed expenditure* for a business to be sustainable and that *optimising profit to achieve a sustainable return on investment* is crucial. Having those two factors in place is axiomatic for any business to be sustainable – a clear case of 'doing what works'. And equally, it 'really matters' that a business is profitable and that income exceeds expenditure.

However, the conscious leader is ever mindful that if and when *maximising* rather than *optimising* profitability becomes the overriding consideration, the disregarding of other vital issues will inevitably occur. When that happens, undesirable practices sweep in and dominate the organisation. *Short-term-ism* rules the thinking of the leadership. The unbalanced pursuit of profits will ultimately fail (in several ways) in the hands of the very people obsessed with it. Such a narrow approach would feature prominently in a 'What Doesn't Work' list.

Littering the corporate landscape is the debris of such businesses, large and small. One high-profile example is Enron. The leaders' thinking – doing what they thought worked, in total disregard of doing what matters – destroyed the business and negatively impacted tens of thousands of individuals.

The collective thinking of the big four banks in Australia (and other financial institutions), while not destroying them, is also an example of pursuing profits at the expense of the greater good and ultimately at the enormous cost to the reputations and the bottom line of the businesses involved. So, while profitability and ensuring that income exceeds expenditure is vital, it is only one such ingredient to be kept at the forefront of our thinking when leading a business.

As stated, I wrote this to my son in the early 2000s. What I said then about my experience of parts of the corporate world turned out to be a gross understatement! I didn't scratch the surface. The criminal, greedy, inhumane behaviour exposed by the 2019 Royal Commission into Misconduct in the Banking, Superannuation and Financial Services Industry turned out to be endemic – far worse than I'd realised.

Because of their relationship with our Federal Government, the level of Government protection they receive, and their central role in our economy, financial institutions have been viewed by many as the custodians of corporate integrity. What surfaced month after month shocked our nation. The level of wrongdoing by the leaders of Australia's most substantial financial institutions still astounds.

IN A STATE OF POSSIBILITY, WE *SEE* HOW TO CONVERGE 'WHAT WORKS' WITH 'WHAT MATTERS'

Let's turn to point four as our example from the 'What Matters' list: '**High-quality working relationships** – people relating to each other as friends, colleagues and co-workers. Supporting each other in getting the job done and achieving the outcomes of the organisation.'

Few would argue that quality working relationships really matter and really work for the business or organisation in many ways: increased productivity, enhanced customer relationships and an improved bottom line are three that immediately come to mind.

On the other hand, unprofessional relationships will result in affairs, gossiping, mucking around, time-wasting with endless storytelling, personal boundaries transgressed, clients ignored and entire departments becoming unproductive. You probably have personal examples in your own working life where this has occurred.

Once mutual respect is lost, high-quality working relationships break down. Some symptoms are: workers arrive late, leave early and don't give a damn about delivering the promise of the enterprise.

While high-quality relationships 'matter' and are at the heart of sustainable businesses and organisations, the conscious leader tunes into recognising poor-quality relationships masquerading as the other. Consider the following:

- Both the benefits and limitations of 'what we think works' and 'what we think matters' are revealed to us when *seen* from The Realm of Possibility.

- We *see* that 'what we think works' and 'what we think matters' only ever works and only ever matters over the long term if our decisions and actions come from the state of awareness that manifests kindness, understanding, wisdom and common sense.

The convergence of 'what works' and 'what matters' is the only sustainable way forward.

WHERE DO YOU SIT RIGHT NOW?

What do you make of all this? Importantly, which one of the types do you feel best describes you? If you're unsure, consider how each type would view the content of this chapter:

- **The Producer** – an archetypal 'what works' Producer, having no time to waste on such matters, would have thrown this letter aside after the opening paragraph, thinking there is no place in business or probably anywhere else for this BS! A more self-aware Producer would *see* that production – meaning, in NLV's case, more harmonious and thus more sustainable communities springing up – is being driven by demand for the lifestyle enjoyed by the NLV lifestylers. He or she would also recognise that a more harmonious environment would free up organisational resources as a result of the lifestylers becoming increasingly self-managing, making the business more profitable and sustainable.

- **The Administrator** – an archetypal 'what works' Administrator would read this as a duty and be preoccupied with thinking about where there might be proven examples of these concepts having worked before, how much it might cost to implement such ideas, and how to control such fanciful notions. A more self-aware Administrator would *see* that management costs would be cut, effectiveness increased and profits improved with self-managed, self-sustaining, self-propagating, self-promoting communities. He or she would see that while controls are important, self-control is the ultimate form.

- **The Entrepreneur** – an archetypal 'what matters' Entrepreneur could very well think this is THE ANSWER and introduce it straight away, without thinking it through – certainly without allowing sufficient resources to test the idea and seeing if the testing demonstrated its effectiveness. A more self-aware Entrepreneur would *see* how, if soundly implemented, this would set NLV apart from its competitors and give the company a great point of difference. One aspect of difference, and marketing advantage, would be in existing happy lifestylers talking in glowing terms with prospective new residents on village open days. Equally, NLV would be attracting top staff as a result of this friendly, inviting, inclusive culture. Again, the result would be to foster business growth profitability and sustainability.

- **The Integrator** – an archetypal 'what matters' Integrator would likely recoil at the heady nature of business-speak, profit motives and the heavy emphasis on commercial success. At the same time, Integrators – drawn to people-oriented concepts like kindness, understanding, wisdom and common sense – would be very curious. He or she could be in a quandary (as Integrators so often are), thinking this was just another attempt by capitalists to manipulate, control and take advantage of consumers. A more self-aware Integrator would *see* that creating genuinely sustainable communities would deliver the NLV promise to lifestylers as nothing else could and achieve a new level of sustainable community and integration throughout the whole organisation. NLV would become truly client-centred, thus ensuring its success and sustainability.

- **The Dead Wood** – an archetypal Dead Wood leader would be saying something like, 'Here we go again. We've tried everything, "nothing works" and "nothing matters", and here is more crap to put up with.' Once a manager has reached this state of mind, his or her thinking has atrophied and is lost to society unless a Copernican revolution takes place in their head and creates a massive change of heart. If this occurs, welcome back to The Realm of Possibility and contributing to the common good!

AND THERE'S MORE

Taking the ideas presented here a step further, there exists a more conscious leader, a self-aware individual living and working from a state of Possibility beyond the archetypal five stereotypes but still with a propensity towards being like one of the first four.

The conscious leader embraces both 'doing what works' and 'doing what matters' in their organisational life. They operate from the context of *'what really works'* and *'what really matters'*, and *see* from the perspective of all five leaders above – including Dead Wood. Everyone has a contribution to make, even if only to make us *aware* of 'what's not working' and 'what isn't *seen* to matter'.

Well, Son, I have laid out an approximation of how I see the psychological and philosophical context in which NLV as an organisation lives, works and might respond to its clients and therefore to the marketplace. The next part of this letter details how your stated purpose of enriching the lives of lifestylers might be significantly enhanced while simultaneously improving the bottom line and dramatically growing the desirability of NLV as a lifestyle choice for increasing numbers of over-45-year-olds.

PART TWO: CREATING AND SUSTAINING HARMONIOUS COMMUNITIES WITHIN EACH VILLAGE SO PEOPLE ARE ENCOURAGED TO *SEE* POSSIBILITY

'A harmonious culture fosters further harmony.'

NLV has a stated commitment to creating excellent internal and external communications. Even so, with growth, slippage is inevitable. Breakdowns occur, and remedial action becomes harder as habits of thinking (beliefs, opinions, judgements and habitual ways of looking at the business) become entrenched, causing failures in communications and relationships.

If a visionary model is not introduced (in keeping with your vision for NLV) for creating sustainable community, then, because of the nature of the NLV business, as you continue to grow, the organisation may find sustainability much more difficult or perhaps even impossible as the lines of communication become longer and the bandwidth for reaching people becomes narrower.

In summary, the following says: any business that commits to living, working and delivering goods or services in a context of *'what really works and what really matters'* – a state of Possibility (i.e. kindness, understanding, wisdom and common sense) – will be sustainable.

Unless creating sustainable community is embraced by the board and staff of NLV, the business will fail to achieve its optimal potential. At best, it will operate at a level below what is essential for it to thrive as an organisation. At worst, it could fail. More to the point, as the hosts of the villages, you would be out of sync with your lifestylers if you decide to introduce the suggested program for them but not enter into a similar one for yourselves. In effect, saying to the residents, 'do as we say, not as we do' will fail, as any wise person will attest. You can't create a sustainable environment for your clients if you can't create one for yourself.

Providing and implementing such a model for the entire NLV team is not only desirable, it's essential. Doing so is beyond the scope of this letter, but there is no escaping that requirement, should you decide to proceed with this or some other form of creating a sustainable community. A specially designed program for the company would be along the same lines as that created for the villagers. We're all people looking for a supportive community.

THE EVOLUTION OF SUSTAINABLE NLV COMMUNITIES USING VILLAGE CIRCLES

A Village Circle is a group of 10 to 15 village residents meeting regularly to converse. Introducing Village Circles to NLV holds the potential to create sustainable relationships within the resident populations and among NLV personnel. In such Circles, lifestylers may participate on a regular, planned basis, speak from their hearts, listen deeply to each other and thus, with time and excellent group facilitation, be indeed *seen* and *heard*.

Sounds simple, right? It is! However, it takes time, coaching of the Circle members and conscious facilitation. The operational success of the

Village Circle model lies in the following seven simple ideas. Based on the philosophy, human dynamics, and the understanding of Thought (The Realms of both Possibility and impossibility), they will work and matter. The purpose of each idea is to create a context for authentic dialogue and sustainable relationships *within* each and *between* each village and the NLV company members. The following seven points are essential ingredients:

1. The active involvement of sufficient numbers of village lifestylers in the Village Circle process.

2. The heartfelt intention, commitment and support of the NLV board, management and staff in introducing a pilot Village Circle to their communities.

3. Providing the pilot is successful, the ongoing commitment and support of the board, senior management and staff to Village Circles are integral to the sustainability of the Circles.

4. The efficacy of the philosophy, protocols and methodologies used in training participants and convening the Circles that foster sustainable relationships.

5. The quality of training the members of the pilot Village Circle receive in understanding its purpose and process. Establishing the pilot to function as intended is critical to those that follow.

6. The selection, maturity, training, skill and capacity of the convenor of each Circle.

7. The ongoing availability of a suitable venue in each village for lifestylers to meet for the Circle.

THE SEVEN IDEAS FLESHED OUT

1. If there were insufficient lifestylers interested in participating in the initial training (the pilot group), the Village Circle idea would lapse. The most precise determinant of the value or otherwise of a Circle is the level of interest among potential participants in its formation and ongoing usefulness in supporting the sustainability of the community.

2. In setting up the pilot Village Circle, the NLV board, management and staff would need to hold and sustain the intention and motivation of allowing the naturally inherent goodwill (the kind,

understanding, wise and common-sense nature) of people being realised and nurtured. If, on the other hand, the intention or motivation is to facilitate or lead the lifestylers into compliance or trouble-free behaviour, then the concept won't work. Any form of manipulation (a not-infrequent occurrence in business/organisational group facilitation) or coercion (leading a group with control in mind) is as distant from what I'm pointing towards as the Sun is from Earth.

3. NLV is developing sustainability models for the physical environment of each new village. This letter is the <u>first draft</u> of a model for creating a sustainable community within the lifestyler populations. It addresses the psychological/sociological well-being of lifestylers as members of a sustainable NLV community. As a landmark concept, it will need the board, management and staff of NLV to understand and embrace the process fully. All tiers of NLV leadership will need to understand the value of having self-managed, self-sustaining communities in each village for the ongoing sustainability of the NLV business model. They would need to recognise that this approach, if successful, would take NLV to a new level of operational ease and excellence while manifestly increasing its attractiveness to potential lifestylers.

4. The philosophy, protocols and methodologies to be used in setting up and convening the Circles and the format for the initial session will be provided in detail should this idea move forward.

5. At the heart of what we are proposing is the role of facilitating the Circles. Critical to the success of the Village Circles is for the facilitator to be in a state of kindness (a warm feeling of connectedness and goodwill), understanding (exploring and comprehending without judgement), wisdom (acting from vision and *insight*), and common sense (an understanding of life and the human condition).

6. For this sustainable community model to 'really work and really matter', my experience is that the convenor of each Circle should meet the following criteria:

    - Be 50 or older.

    - Demonstrate in their daily life that they already have a high level of listening capability and engagement with others.

- See the possibilities for fostering harmonious, sustainable community by utilising the concept of the Village Circle.
- See the value to themselves and others of developing sustainable relationships in the village.
- Be willing to undertake additional, separate and ongoing convenor training.

7. A suitable venue within each village would be:
   - a quiet place;
   - private for 4 hours;
   - available for a regular, scheduled day and time;
   - equipped with comfortable chairs;
   - air-conditioned;
   - set up with self-serve tea and coffee facilities;
   - within easy access to toilets.

CRITICAL STEPS IN SETTING UP THE PILOT AND VILLAGE CIRCLES

- Finding lifestylers (say, 15) who support the concept of a Village Circle would be ideal in getting the first trial Circle in motion.
- An invitation would be sent to every resident, containing sufficient information about a Village Circle and inviting those interested to a meeting outlining the purpose and process.
- This meeting would outline the philosophy of the Village Circle in some detail, then have a question time.
- We would ask for volunteers to attend a training program. If more than 15 apply, a ballot would determine the participants for the first training weekend.
- Based on a satisfactory outcome from the training weekend, a trial Village Circle of 12 x 4-hour sessions would take place.
- Based on the success or otherwise of the weekend training and subsequent trial Village Circle, the project will either proceed in

the existing form, be modified (if considered wise) or lapse if the trial failed to achieve the outcomes sought.

- The training weekend would cover the creation and maintenance of a sustainable community, including, but not limited to, the following:

    i. **The Circle:** The Circle has been used throughout human history when people want to speak in an environment of equality. Every member of the Circle can see and be seen by each member. Listening in the Circle is made more accessible by seeing each speaker's face and body language. There is neither a beginning nor an end to the Circle, no physical hierarchy or privileged place.

    ii. **Listening:** A listening program designed to suit the lifestylers will be a central part of the training weekend. The essence of this training will teach lifestylers to:

    - be attentive and quiet when another member speaks;
    - let go of their thoughts and listen with an open mind and heart even when what is said is not consistent with their own beliefs, opinions, judgments and knowledge;
    - be genuinely open, i.e., neither agree nor disagree with what is being said by others in the Circle, but be engaged;
    - listen attentively and respectfully, not interrupting, acknowledging the speaker when he or she has finished, and waiting for some seconds before the next person speaks;
    - eventually experience deep and unconditional listening, which is **the crucial element** of the Village Circle;
    - understand the point and purpose of the Village Circle: that being SEEN and being HEARD is a wonderful experience for people. Being able to give voice to our thoughts and feelings in a safe environment is liberating, uplifting and beneficial to our psychological and physical wellbeing. When

we are indeed seen and heard, we feel accepted, and move into more profound and more positive feelings of warmth (kindness), compassion (understanding), perspective (wisdom) and discernment (common sense).

DOES A VILLAGE CIRCLE HELP CREATE SUSTAINABLE COMMUNITY?

The success of the Village Circle model lies in lifestylers' living and relating to one another in a state of Possibility. How is that achieved? Have you ever tried to describe the taste and texture of a sweet ripe mango to someone who has never eaten one? Trying to convey what occurs within individuals in such a Circle is about as challenging.

Transformation doesn't come from the application of any technique, exercise or even from the process. While tried and tested facilitation skills are utilised, and the entire program is a process, the effect experienced by members occurs within the awareness of each person when they shift into a state of Possibility.

The Village Circle is a simple idea yet potentially profound in its impact. It is not 'touchy-feely' and does not invade the private space of any individual. It is not preaching, but it is self-educational in that it encourages people to quieten their minds, to become more reflective and to access their inner resources and more profound understanding and awareness of themselves and others.

A naturally occurring outcome, from the way the Circle convenes (coming together in a particular way over the weeks), is that each member progresses at their rate through the following stages:

Weeks 1 – 3: Certain individuals, trying to assert themselves, command more time and space, are more vocal and sometimes more demanding. Others begin to feel they belong in the Circle and are comfortable with what's unfolding. Others still, not being willing to compete with the more robust, may withdraw from the conversation and consider leaving the group. All minds tend to be busy in these early meetings. The convenor needs to display kindness, understanding, wisdom and common sense to hold the space for all. None of this is right or wrong. It is merely part of the inevitable process.

Weeks 3 – 5: Some members will observe that more time and opportunity to be heard by the less vocal and less assertive within the Circle is needed. They will assist these members to emerge. Some anxiety will be experienced in the group as a little human jostling takes place. Many minds are still busy. Some are starting to quieten and embrace what they are hearing and seeing unfold, and the potential benefit to the common good of the village community.

Weeks 5 – 8: The group is now starting to blend, and most members are making a more even contribution to the conversation. The dialogue is more intimate (more real, less superficial) and relevant to more individuals. More minds are calming, and some are becoming quiet and reflective.

Weeks 8 – 11: By now, the group is starting to function in a very supportive and kind way for all members. There is a growing understanding of the differences in personality and an embracing of the diversity of various backgrounds and cultures. The quality of listening is vastly improved. Minds are calmer now, many are quiet, and some participants will experience a profound sense of peace within and beyond the Circle.

Weeks 11 – 15: Many members of the Circle have moved into a personal space of quiet, deep listening and reflection. Minds are calm, the majority quiet, and more are experiencing peace. Members readily access their innate kindness, understanding, wisdom and common sense, the state of awareness that *'really works and really matters'* in creating and sustaining community.

Beyond week 15: Some members will be experiencing levels of heartfelt intimacy never felt before. The result of this newfound level of functioning will manifest in many ways. From my experience of facilitating Circles, these ways include:

- Self-awareness will have grown. Beliefs, opinions and judgements about life and others will become more apparent to each participant. This lifetime-held conditioning is *seen* as simply 'learned prejudices'. These blocks to a sustainable community begin to loosen up and fall away.

- Thoughts and feelings of separation will be changing to thoughts and feelings of connectedness. Importantly, these will spill over to village life beyond the Circle.

- As the levels of self-awareness rise within the Circle, members move towards a level of personal conscious leadership. The usual sources of discontent, such as petty annoyances, rivalries and misplaced upsets possibly directed towards NLV, along with all manner of human irritants, start to give way to kindness, understanding, wisdom and common sense.

- The listening of each other in the Village Circle will see the emergence of the authentic self. Members find their real voice.

- At this point, a member of the group will likely step forward to facilitate a new group within the village while still maintaining membership of their original group.

WHY VILLAGE CIRCLES 'WILL WORK' AND 'WILL MATTER' TO THOSE INVOLVED

The Village Circle <u>will work because it matters</u> to people that they live in a safe, supportive community – a place where they feel they belong. That is one significant reason NLV has been as successful as it has been to date. Most of the physical-safety issues are accommodated in the design and management of each village.

The Village Circle concept holds the potential for living in a National Lifestyle Village to go to a new level, further enriching the lives of each resident and the community as a whole. This latent potential is due to the psychological and social issues – which each lifestyler creates – and the influence they have on each other, so residents feel nurtured in a safe and straightforward manner. This will strongly complement the safety their physical environment offers.

Moreover, the long-term impact of embracing Village Circles holds the potential for NLV communities to become increasingly self-managed. The cost of managing villages becomes lower than in similar organisations. Village Circles would be a powerful and unique element of the NLV business model.

The Village Circle <u>will matter because it would work</u> in creating a Circle, or Circles, of lifestylers that would contribute to the following:

- The opportunity for any resident to give voice to and to be heard on any issue, and thus have a powerful and positive influence on the psychological and social wellbeing of the whole village community.

- More specifically, the Village Circle would provide a forum for every Circle member to give voice and listened to on any matter, from joy and happiness to concern and upset. It would be the ideal forum for suggesting any improvements to the village and thus eliminate the need for counterproductive gossiping or intrigue among lifestylers. It would alleviate a 'them and us' attitude.
- The Village Circle would serve to assist lifestylers in clarifying their thinking and ensuring their decisions come from a context of kindness, understanding, wisdom and common sense.

THE POTENTIAL IMPACT OF CIRCLES ON NATIONAL LIFESTYLE VILLAGES AND THE NLV CORPORATION

- As a likely result of each Circle member's shift in awareness, they would relate to each other and to the world outside the Circle from a growing state of kindness, understanding, wisdom and common sense – *what really works and what really matters* in creating a sustainable community.
- The village culture would change with the healthier and happier perspectives of Circle members.
- Similarly impacted would be the relations with NLV management and staff.
- Consequently, the costs of managing a National Lifestyle Village would fall as the desirability of living there would rise.

Son, what more could any client ask of their provider? What more could any business leader ask of their clients?

Reference Material

(1) Hull D & Read V 2003, 'Simply the Best', working paper, University of New South Wales.
(2) I Adizes 1979, *How To Solve The Mismanagement Crisis: Diagnosis and Treatment of Management Problems*, Adizes Institute, San Diego.

CHAPTER 5

THE CAREER, BUSINESS AND COMMERCIAL GAME

Being truly in service is a state of Possibility.

When we are out of touch with Possibility, we become lost in 'The Game of Living'. What follows illustrates one of the games of living we play and the unintended consequences when we get lost in it and see it as 'the truth'. It's a game most of us play to some degree.

Working for others or ourselves is just a game. It's an essential game for most, a way to put food on the table, a roof over our heads, and pay the increasing bill load of modern families. It can also be a way to challenge ourselves and make a contribution to the common good. For some, it's perhaps a way to achieving fame and fortune.

This game (like all the games of living we play out) means different things to different people. Some revel in it, some dislike it, some think of it as a necessity, and others simply reject its premise entirely as a blot on society.

Played from the spirit of Possibility, this game makes a positive contribution.

Played simply for money or power, this particular game can be destructive, desperate and dirty. Playing this way will negatively affect staff, customers, shareholders, community, government, the environment, the economy and future generations.

Experiencing and playing the career, business and commercial game from our state of impossibility separates players from their deeper connection with Life and The Realm of Possibility. It becomes a game of *all about me and mine*. If our identity becomes tied to success and accumulation, we miss seeing Possibility.

Playing this game from Possibility ensures that it fulfils its role in our society and contributes to the common good, as fleshed out elsewhere in this guide.

BEING IN SERVICE IS 'DELIVERING THE PROMISE'

For some reading this guide, it may seem as if a business influenced by Possibility means flying without a compass or rudder. From another perspective, one may notice essential themes and practical imperatives. A critical one of the latter is that of *being in service* and *delivering the promise*.

Possibility and being in service go together; they're doorways to each other. Implicit in working in any organisation, whether self-employed or employed by another, is an implied promise. That promise is simple: *my job is to be in service to the customer, client or patient to whom I am offering my goods, services or care. I will deliver on that promise at all times to the best of my ability and capacity.*

Having this understanding is at the heart of being successful. Successful in whatever we undertake – from brain surgery to fruit-picking, cleaning to astrophysics.

Development programs aimed at raising service standards do their best to deliver on that promise. In my experience, many fail in their endeavour. The unrecognised reason for their failure is that the core aspects of the Fourth Element – Thought and its states of Possibility and impossibility – are not understood and therefore not addressed.

Without that understanding, the results of any training are hit-and-miss at best and, at worst, counterproductive. Those that don't need the training may benefit by learning some new skills. Those that are regularly blinded by their impossibility thinking will most likely not be touched.

Being in service may not be a priority for some or even any members of a business or organisation. If that consciousness is not already awake in individuals, skill training seems not to help. The information delivered will be simply more information piled on an already overloaded and resistant mind. That is, unless the inherent value of being in service strikes home within the awareness of the individual. That is left to happenstance unless our states of mind are specifically explored.

Instead of pointing us toward the state of awareness and thus the change of heart required for being in service, programs often deliver ideas on how to manipulate behaviour – our own or others'. Such approaches ask us to act as if we care when we don't, or use clever, tried and tested language that can coerce or manipulate clients into taking action that isn't necessarily in their best interests.

Sometimes such training programs end up being the catalyst for despair, ill will and failure, with participants never getting to understand the critical importance of being in heartfelt service. They never *see* how our state of awareness determines what we deliver – heartfelt or otherwise.

We can *pretend* to be in service, or we can *actually* be in service. We either have the feeling of goodwill, or we don't.

The defining difference in each of our attitudes to customers/clients/patients (and everyone else in our life) boils down to answering this (rather long) question. Are we in a state of service, delivering the implicit promise of the business or organisation we represent – and do we continue to do so irrespective of whether the owner, manager, our co-workers and those we serve and serve with have an understanding that such a promise exists?

'DELIVERING THE PROMISE' RESULTS FROM BEING IN SERVICE

As already pointed to, it's a commonly shared belief both in the worlds of business and psychology that by teaching good service behaviours or by sharing good ideas (*any* practices or good ideas – like reading this book), we will experience a fundamental shift, and transform our attitude.

I put to you that changing behaviours is very hit and miss. Consider some of the amazingly powerful books you've read and how compelling the content was. Did you experience a sustained shift in your consciousness as a consequence?

Teaching better behaviours or trying to instil new and more appropriate ideas allows only for a superficial and temporary change, if that. It's much like transferring water from one vessel to another: the shape and space are changed but not the actual make-up.

Truly being in service goes hand in glove with our innate philosophy of living and is consistent with our core attitude towards our fellow man. Being in service exists within each of us, but we must discover it there.

What we need to address then is how to get in touch with our core philosophy, the one inherent in every human being, the one we are born with – love, understanding, wisdom and common sense. Being in that state of service generates a remarkable feeling – a feeling that has us giving of our heart. That is because it is who we are, in essence, a reflection of our innate wholeness. We have not just changed vessels; when we experience Possibility, we 'turn water into wine'.

I hear some of you ask; 'What value does this BS have in the real world?' 'In a dog-eat-dog marketplace, the world of hard-nosed organisations and ruthless competition, can we afford to be in service?' 'What if I work for a manager who doesn't give a damn? One who sees clients as "fair game" to be fleeced?'

We can look at its intrinsic worth and its commercial value by looking at three ordinary people working in real estate, an industry that, in theory, is all about being in service to clients. We'll explore the thinking of these real-estate agents.

At the same time, I'm asking you to contrast their thinking and behaviour with the way you might think, and how your thinking in that state would influence the service you would deliver. And more broadly, reflect on how your state of awareness would impact on your life in general. Let's *see* if you can recognise yourself in all three states.

THE THREE FACES OF SERVICE

In each state, let's imagine our job (and, it follows, hand in glove, our life in general) very differently. In each case, we will see how these different states of mind determine the service we provide and the quality of our life in each state. In the first example, we are an agent 'out of service'; in the second we are 'providing conditional service'; in the third, we are 'being in service' or what I love to call 'delivering the promise' – these latter two terms used interchangeably.

I could draw examples from any and every field: clergymen to mayors; lawyers to people on the checkout; shearers to teachers; plumbers to professors. The same is true for each of us when we *see* what being in service truly means. We could even look at various shades between these three states of mind – but the point, I trust, will be clear.

Real-estate agents have a job that throws up unique challenges. That is why I picked them. Most who try it don't succeed. Agents work odd and often extended hours in meeting the demands of their clients – sellers, buyers, and those just 'having a look'. Add to that fierce competition, often-difficult market conditions and all the usual demands of being in business, you come up with a job that by its nature demands a lot.

The Three Service States of Mind

FIRST: I AM 'OUT OF SERVICE'

I'm certain I know how the world works, but never stop to wonder why it doesn't work so well for me.

When 'out of service' in dealing with the listing, sale and/or purchase of a property, I see the client as an obstacle to overcome, not a partner in a mutually rewarding undertaking.

My focus is on how much commission is in the deal and how quickly and easily the deal can be done. With little or no joy in my work and relationships, my *modus operandi* is to achieve the desired outcome with the least possible input and effort.

In this state of mind, I avoid interactions with my client. I don't understand that my approach, in their reality, is working against my aim of earning commission. As strange as it sounds, I'm unable to connect the dots between the quality of my input and an optimal outcome for the seller, the buyer and me.

My attitude towards the customer might be summarised as 'putting up with the bastards'. Day-to-day my feelings run the gamut of stress, anxiety, resentment and often anger. Underlying these emotions is my fear of not getting the listing or the sale, and thus the commission.

In dealing with this hollow existence, my coping mechanisms include alcohol or drugs, gambling and having affairs. Because I don't have a sense of peace in my life, these are methods I use to experience a 'nice feeling'. They are short-lived, self-destructive, and I need more and more of these 'remedies' to fill the growing void in my experience of the life I'm living.

My job, as you can imagine, becomes increasingly tough over time as my work and life habits deteriorate. Sleeping in late, taking in a movie during work hours, long lunches with more drink than food, or hiding behind paperwork in the office are also common practices for me.

I find anything preferable to actually being in service because I don't know the intrinsic value of being so to myself or my clients. Working under such mental strain, I avoid keeping my buyer or seller up to date on progress.

You might question my longevity operating in this mode. Surprisingly, some of us survive and a few of us (the clever, cunning and manipulative) can be successful, albeit only in material terms. The personal cost to my relationships and to me is huge.

Most of us entering real estate, often because we think it's an easy path to a high income, don't start at the far end of being 'out of service', although some do. If, as a new agent entering the field, I don't understand what state of mind it takes to deliver the promise (this applies equally to any field of endeavour), I may well finish up out of service.

Because I don't *see* that my state of mind is (and always has been) my problem, in being out of service, I will blame the nature of the industry. I'll hold market conditions, the company I work for, responsible, and I will especially lay blame with my clients – those 'bastards' – the buyer or seller.

If it is suggested to me, I consider 'delivering the promise' and being in heartfelt service as 'Pollyanna-ish'.

Maybe being in service simply lies in an unknown state of mind, one I haven't experienced or one I have lost sight of.

SECOND: I PROVIDE 'CONDITIONAL SERVICE'

If the service I provide is conditional, is it really being in service?

In providing 'conditional service', I recognise my customers as being important. Yes, I realise that without them I would not earn a living. My attitude is one of doing the best I can in the light of the prevailing circumstances and coping as best I can with people's failings.

I know I must provide good service or lose out. My level of understanding is often described as 'enlightened self-interest'. The emphasis is, nevertheless, on *self*-interest. However, I don't understand the deeper point behind that phrase.

Some of the everyday feelings I may experience are:

- great excitement at success;
- deep disappointment at failure;
- stress from the effort it takes to maintain conditional service;
- indignation and hurt when customers don't respond positively to my efforts;
- a sense that I am often at the mercy of others.

For about the first year, I enjoyed my job, but find it tougher and tougher as time rolls by. Increasingly, I'm experiencing what is euphemistically called 'burnout' and, if I endure, I sense I'll become bitter and cynical, and finally leave the industry.

Or worse, I will shift into the 'out of service' state of mind, a state that I notice some in the industry are in. And if somehow I manage to maintain some reasonable perspective on other aspects of my life, the pleasure in my job will fade to zero. Pleasure in my job is giving way to going through the daily motions or carrying on through sheer hard grind and self-discipline.

To maintain some semblance of a decent life, I've developed life-coping mechanisms such as working out at the gym, jogging, yoga, meditation or reading self-help books.

I'm unaware of the state of 'delivering the promise'. If I do glimpse it, I don't understand what it is and therefore can't readily access it. If I move into that state of mind for a day to two, I'm not aware of what's occurring in a way where it leads to a transformation of my experience of my job and my life.

Note: In addition to the high percentage of real-estate agents that fall into these first two categories, many of us within our own field of endeavour fall into them as well. Whether we are a nurse or a courier, it doesn't make any difference. Particularly in Australia, we fall short on being in service, and there is much conversation about this. Not to mention the mountain of commercial material written about the poor quality of service offered and the large training industry that has developed trying to improve it. As said, it is ironic that we who complain so much about poor service mostly fall into these two categories within our own work, even within our relationships. Being on the receiving end of poor service doesn't mean we wake up and see the source of being in service – that state of awareness where we naturally, without thinking, 'deliver the promise'.

THIRD: BEING 'IN SERVICE'

Delivering the promise requires us to have the same attitude of goodwill towards everyone; it also means not counting the cost.

Being fortunate enough to be 'in service' and 'delivering the promise', we experience our job and life from an entirely different vantage point. We regard the customer and those near and dear – and humanity in general – with respect and understanding. Being in service, we seldom complain about the customer; when we do, we catch ourselves and feel a touch of chagrin. We know that we too are a perfectly flawed human being who also has low moods and 'stuffs up' from time to time.

And we are grateful that we have joined the dots and now understand that the quality of our thinking is the sole determinant of our sense of wellbeing and our capacity to be in service. We acknowledge that our thinking reflects Possibility or impossibility and is not a reflection of our circumstances.

In general, our attitude is one of goodwill and generosity of spirit. We recognise and embrace the big things we need to do, and equally embrace the little things with the same diligence, commitment and enthusiasm. Our working context is that, while it is important to get the big deal or attend to the lucrative customer, it is as important to sort out the small after-sale matter with an aged pensioner or assist the client wanting to rent an inexpensive unit (even if rentals are 'not our department').

For us, being in service isn't determined by the amount of money involved, rather it is determined by our core values: kindness and understanding and the level of wisdom and common sense we experience. We don't need coping mechanisms, as we recognise that the source of any stress or upset starts and finishes with us. We're it. And knowing that it is the quality of our thinking at any point in time that enables us to maintain our bearings, and if perchance we lose them, we know how to recover quickly.

We are a doorway, not a doormat. Being 'in service' doesn't mean we are obliged to take on everyone's problems, be burdened with copious detail or assume others' responsibilities. Neither is it an invitation for anyone to wipe their feet on us. But, even if not within our ambit, we will ensure that a customer, client or inquirer is introduced to another member of our team whose job it is to take care of that person. And we will make certain that, that person will be, and is, looked after.

Evaluating, comparing, contrasting and minutely counting the costs of service are not part of our life. For us, going the proverbial extra mile is just another mile, a natural occurrence, nothing out of the ordinary. It is not a big deal. It is just the way we live in assisting and supporting our fellow traveller on our own journey of living.

In 'delivering the promise' we are appreciative of our job, the organisation we represent, and the industry we are a part of. Cynicism, hard-heartedness and ill will are not part of our experience. Goodwill, feelings of gratitude and connectedness are everyday thoughts and feelings we have.

As said, we do not need coping devices to maintain our bearings or to stay sane. We recognise stress for what it is: a state of mind in which we take life too seriously, where we are preoccupied with the outcome or fretting about the past, rather than enjoying the process in each moment of Possibility (actual or potential).

We *see* that our view of our job has nothing to do with the prevailing conditions, circumstances or the amount of business on hand or lack thereof. By being in service, we are generally light-hearted and filled with good feelings. Our mind is a doorway to a better experience of life.

Being truly in service is a state of Possibility.

KEY DISTINCTIONS BETWEEN THESE THREE STATES OF MIND

When we lose our connection with Possibility – with Life – we become lost in 'The Game of Living'.

OUT OF SERVICE

We are stuck in our habit of dysfunctional thinking – a state of impossibility. Like a car with serious mechanical problems and in need of a major overhaul, we splutter along, often making a lot of noise.

Self-absorbed, calculating and ruminating, our mind is troubled and seldom at rest. We are constantly distracted by thoughts such as 'What's in this for me?', 'This is a bloody nuisance, I have already called him five times long-distance', 'How can I get them to do the deal right now?', 'I don't care who pays for this stuff-up, so long as it's not me.' This line of thinking is our daily diet. Lost in our conditioning, our thinking is of poor quality, to say the least.

Annoyance, frustration and judgement hound us.

PROVIDING CONDITIONAL SERVICE

We are like a car requiring a good tune-up before it can run smoothly again. Far from broken down, it can still do the job, but burns more fuel, leaks oil and shows signs of wear and tear. It has become far less pleasurable to drive.

We innocently think we know which side our bread is buttered on. Our mind is busy and analytical. Worry is a regular companion. Hurt feelings or disappointment occur regularly. For example: we take it personally and get upset when a sale falls through or our clients give their property to another agent to handle. Our thinking runs along these lines: 'They don't appreciate how hard I've tried'; 'What do you have to do to please some people?'; 'Life isn't fair'; 'I have to be on my guard'; 'People are fine but they will let you down'; 'I must sacrifice or fail'.

We recognise to some extent – certainly more than agents in the first example – that we are at cause in making our experience of life difficult. To assist ourselves, we tend to read the latest motivational book or display posters that say, 'The tough get going when the going gets tough'; 'Go the extra mile'; 'Smile and the world smiles with you, cry and you cry alone'. We don't realise that we are influenced for only a moment by reading a positively worded poster, and then only at a very superficial level.

We haven't reached that state of awareness where we *see* that our thoughts and feelings are internally generated, and not caused as a result of what the client may or may not say or do in relation to us. Nor do we realise that *we can't be deeply impacted* by reading a guide such as this until we *see* beyond the words and *see* Possibility for ourselves.

We might well be into positive thinking, affirmations and similar ideas (see the section, 'Some popular mental-training models and possibility'). These may sound the same, but are a world away from how an agent who 'delivers the promise' *sees* life.

Hard work, discipline and exhausting effort are constant companions, and often we are searching for the answer to what ails us. We are on track to having a better experience at work and home but haven't *seen* the primacy of the role of Thought and our thinking, and we don't understand the power and peace revealed within The Realm of Possibility.

Anxiety and stress are often our companions.

DELIVERING THE PROMISE

For us, being in service is simplicity itself. Instead of having to analyse each moment, day, week or year, we take life as it unfolds. Setbacks, rejection, complaints and problems are seldom taken personally unless we lose our bearings, and then we lose them only for a short time.

Nor do we take success and plaudits personally. We *see* everything as life in action, all as impersonal pieces of our life unfolding in whatever way it does.

Our predominant state of awareness is one of gratitude and appreciation. We 'don't sweat the small stuff', and we *see* that all stuff is small stuff. We have what others might describe as a philosophical view of life. As regular visitors to The Realm of Possibility, we may *see* the opportunity and create our own business.

Feelings of gratitude and engagement are common.

THE KEY TO BEING 'IN SERVICE'

In a state of 'delivering the promise', i.e. of 'being in service', we *see* that attitudes (our own and others') are a direct reflection of each person's thinking in the moment, or more deeply, of each person's philosophy of living.

We *see* that our attitude (good, poor or indifferent) is not fixed in stone as result of our upbringing, circumstance or anything external to our capacity to think and create our personal reality in each new moment. We are aware that we can be raised in an 'unsupportive' or 'negative' environment, yet have a 'positive' attitude and, equally, be raised in a 'supportive' or 'positive' environment and have a 'negative' attitude. And we *see* that both are a result of the quality of our thinking in each new moment.

We *see* that our degree of self-awareness and that of every individual is the determinant of our attitude – positive or negative and all shades in between. We also recognise that 'luck', in its infinite manifestations, is not the cause of us gaining or losing a state of inner peace. We understand that what is going on in our mind (what we are thinking) is what creates our personal experience – an experience of peace or inner turmoil and all shades in between.

We are *seeing* or have *seen* into The Realm of Possibility, even though we may not know it by that or any other name. However, we are aware of the 'inside-out nature of the human experience'. We understand that, regardless of how life appears, it is the quality of our thinking, feelings and actions – a state of Possibility or impossibility – that determines whether we are 'in service' or not.

We understand that our reality is an internally generated experience (and is unrelated to our specific circumstances). We *see* that it is Thought at cause in generating our feelings, whether happy or sad, peaceful or desperate, creative or *status quo,* open to Possibility or closed to it.

We who deliver the promise experience life events with a very neutral view. Setbacks, rejection, misadventure, or acknowledgment and a run of successes or failures are all *seen* with an understanding of neutrality and held lightly. As a consequence, we enjoy our job and life in general.

We *see* that our experience of life, our personal reality, is what we create from the gift of Thought. That while there may be a physical reality, a set of circumstances out there, our personal experience of life, the way we see or *see* any set of circumstances, is always exclusive to us. Our reality is 100-percent subjective – our creation alone. Our personal reality (the only reality we will ever know) is truly an inside-out created process. What we think is what we see or *see*.

THE INSIDE-OUT NATURE OF IT ALL

As we *see* with growing clarity that our moment-to-moment experience is determined by Thought and the quality of our thinking in each millisecond, we become increasingly philosophical. Each new *seeing*, in turn, leads us to become less disturbed, psychologically, by life's sweet whims and relentless unfoldings. This is how Nelson Mandela, after decades in prison, could return to society as the embodiment of kindness, understanding, wisdom and common sense. This is precisely why he was so loved by his people and admired by the world.

As a result, we feel happier more of the time – like Mandela did – and when we don't feel so good, we understand that the cause isn't what is happening in our life but rather what is happening within our head, the thinking we are entertaining.

Happiness, equanimity and a feeling of goodwill and connectedness to our fellow man increasingly become our way of life. This equanimous state of awareness is our natural condition – for all of us human beings to experience when our minds are not fixated on any belief, opinion, judgement or piece of knowledge. For all of us, released from our self-created prison: our conditioned mind.

It is impossible for us to be in healthy psychological functioning and not be in a state of service. It is equally impossible for us to be in an unhealthy state of mind and to be genuinely (not in adapted behaviour) in service and delivering the promise.

Providing 'conditional service' is preferable to being 'out of service', but it's only a thought away from being 'out of service' – *but also* only a thought away from 'delivering the promise'.

Each is a seamless next step. One, you might say, is a step backward (into the past) – if we don't understand the nature of Thought and *see* our thinking for what it is. The other is a step forward (into *seeing what is*).

We, who *see* our personal reality as being internally created, and *see* our imaginings for what they are, enjoy the peace of mind that comes with that understanding. We will naturally be 'in service', as that is who we are, no matter what walk of life we are involved in.

At worst, say, on an off day when our mood is low, we may drop to providing 'conditional service'. We will recognise that our thinking is off and maybe struggle through the motions of being in conditional service. But this increasingly becomes the exception. The more awake we are, the less we are bothered by what is unfolding in our life.

However, we who provide conditional service as learnt behaviour for getting what we want will be at the mercy of our unrecognised thinking and mood swings. On a good day (say, following an inspiring sales meeting) we may be in service and enjoy the wonderful feelings that go with that state. But because we don't understand the inside-out nature of the human experience, we may put it down to circumstances such as a big sale, luck or things just going right – or 'getting out of bed on the right side'.

On an ordinary day our job will be much harder than it need be, and on a bad day (say, following a bad sales meeting or a difficult meeting with a client) we may drop to being 'out of service'.

Whether we are selling real estate, preaching to a flock, working with a jackhammer or CEO of a multinational corporation, being 'in service' is a state of grace.

A state less than that will result in us going through the motions (doing what we know to do) at best, and at worst taking advantage of the implicit trust the client has in us to 'deliver the promise'.

It's Only Natural to Have Expectations. But What If Your Expectations Have You?

Possibility is the realm of conscious leadership.

At our one-on-one coaching session, Keith was very frustrated about a new employee who was not meeting his expectations.

Keith is a young entrepreneur, three years into growing what is fast becoming a very successful organisation. He *sees* Possibility in business, has the attributes necessary to create a great organisation and, importantly, seeks coaching to develop and build on his high-level skills and innate talents.

Even so, his thinking around Raul, the new key position employee, was dense and vexatious – absorbed in impossibility thinking. Keith's impossibility thinking was expressed often, through a variety of statements like:

'I've made a bad decision'.

'He doesn't seem to understand what to do. I can't hold his hand.'

'Raul oversees these men but arrives after they do, what sort of example is that?'

'Should I stop the process right now and sack him – and cut my losses?'

'I have spoken with him, kept my frustration in check and maintained a veneer of rapport. That meeting went okay, but I strongly doubt it will make any difference.'

'His mind is not on the job.'

During our coaching session, Keith began to *see* clearly that the real source of his frustration was his thinking – not Raul's lack of responsiveness. He recognised, at a new level of understanding, his self-admitted judgmental approach. In that recognition his thinking softened.

EXPECTATIONS CAN MORPH AND CONSUME US

Of course, it's appropriate for Keith to have certain expectations of his new employee. That's common sense. However, his disappointment around those expectations was debilitating him. His expectations were in the way of finding positive solutions.

In our coaching session – looking at his internal world, not the external world – Keith revealed that his upset state was relatively constant since Raul started. Gripped by distressed thinking, he had been barely coping – certainly not thriving. Keith recognised that his state of mind was counterproductive. By becoming immersed emotionally in his expectations, he had become part of the problem.

He could now *see* that a more productive approach – influenced from The Realm of Possibility – is to maintain perspective and work towards a mutual solution.

Like all of us, Keith can't change others, only himself.

SEEING POSSIBILITY

During our conversation, his mind had cleared: he *saw* from The Realm of Possibility.

Keith *realised* he had seen the issue with Raul through the memory of his earlier conditioning: from impossibility. That resulted in his set-in-stone thinking, e.g. 'It's my way or the highway.' 'Shape up or ship out!'

By bringing pre-conceived judgments and set beliefs (expectations) to the current situation, Keith had created a binary choice: win or lose. Nothing in-between. But now, realising his thinking was the issue, Keith regained perspective over what he initially thought was an external matter he wanted to control. He felt better, more at ease, heading back towards the top of his game.

With the clarity of thought, Keith could again bring his true talents to his role. He became the conscious leader – not the unconscious boss.

WHAT HAD BEEN GOING ON FOR KEITH?

Keith had been re-living his memory-stored ways of coping, overlaying past thinking on the situation facing him now. He had been creating his reality with the embellishment of his conditioned mind – memories formed decades back.

He habitually dealt with issues in that way. So, he did it again. Which means, he attached all sorts of accumulated meaning to the situation. He was blaming himself: 'I've mucked up.' 'I'm at fault.' 'I'm stupid for employing the wrong person.' And blaming Raul: 'This person's a dickhead'. 'He's hopeless'. 'What's wrong with this jerk?' Keith wasn't *seeing what is* – the reality of a person struggling in his new job.

Instead, in a moment of insight, Keith came to *see* reality, free of the emotional turmoil he had transported through time from his past. Keith realised that impossibility is simply a state of mind. Impossibility is experiencing life through our conditioning, unconsciously applying that pre-set meaning to whatever we are facing right now.

Possibility is also a state of mind. Possibility is *seeing what is*, free of our conditioned thinking (good, bad or indifferent) about whatever we are facing.

SO, WHAT HAPPENED?

Keith's side of the relationship became healthier. Now that he *saw* the storm he had created in his mind, he related to Raul in a much kinder, more understanding, wiser and commonsense way. By *seeing* that his thinking - not Raul's behaviour - was the real cause of his distress, his mental pressure eased. Even more, this internal shift by Keith (the business leader) created the psychological space for Raul (the under-performing employee) to see things more clearly.

Keith was now handling the situation in a way that avoided what could have been an ugly, confrontational situation. Which, among other things, would have created the environment for upset and turmoil among the other staff, affecting the wellbeing of the organisation systemically. Through his clarity of expression and honesty, without emotional distress, Keith was able to offer Raul a clear perspective on his new role. He explained what was needed.

It worked: the situation resolved within days, with both men ultimately respecting the other and each making decisions for the better. (See postscript).

This article could have been about expectations between a parent and child, a couple, or two friends. To have expectations is part of being human. It's when expectations 'have you' that life becomes more complicated and unpleasant than it need be. Living life imbued with Possibility is a far cry from one dominated by impossibility.

Postscript

Just three days into Keith's more enlightened approach, Raul resigned in good grace. He had come to realise he wasn't the right person for the job. He recognised he wasn't up to the task. Gratefully, he had secured a position back at his old firm, but not in the supervisor role he held at Keith's company. He sensibly took a step back to something he thought he could handle at this juncture in his life.

They departed on good terms, and Keith was pleased that Raul had landed on his feet. Keith was encouraged by the way he had turned things around and navigated his way through this challenging leadership situation: with kindness, understanding and common sense – not with protracted harsh judgments, stress and worry.

CHAPTER 6

HOW TO SEE POSSIBILITY USING VERTICAL INQUIRY

Insight is the gateway to transforming your life and everything in it.

'Vertical inquiry' is a form of gentle questioning intended to take a client or workshop attendee beyond their conditioning, to experience a mental stillness and an opening of their access to Possibility. Equally, and with subtlety, it can be utilised in any conversation – with a work colleague or anyone else, for that matter.

The purpose is for the individual to *see* and gain perspective on one or more aspect/s of their life as if for the first time.

It sets out to reveal how *seeing* into The Realm of Possibility within our mind, via a specific questioning process, is particularly useful in leading us to personal insights and a transformed understanding of how we experience reality and of the reality we experience.

What follows contrasts with the more traditional ways of teaching, counselling and coaching, which is to pass on knowledge, including such popular methods as using metaphors, storytelling, analogy, example, case study and all forms of input-focussed instruction. Each of these methods is, to a lesser or greater degree, an 'outside-in approach' to learning. In such an approach, information that is known passes to another, where it might also become known – but this information, as valuable as it might be, is often not learnt in a way that makes a difference in that person's life and relationships.

Our approach to counselling/coaching and how we facilitate The Possibility Workshop directs the participant towards self-discovery, which is an 'inside-out approach' taking the client away from the 'known' and into the 'unknown', and ultimately into The Realm of Possibility – their innate place of true leaning. This experience has the potential to transform forever the life of those being questioned. It can be summed up by: 'Keep asking me relevant questions, and I'll discover within the relevant answer.'

INSIDE-OUT COACHING

As said, traditional teaching/facilitation often gets in the way of discovery. Our coaching approach is based on what this guide suggests, and that is:

- our reality is an internally generated experience;
- specifically, our moment-to-moment reality, experienced through our senses, is brought to us via Thought and perceived through our present level of awareness;
- the wondrous faculty of Thought is the energy that powers each of us in having this miraculous experience called 'our life'.

Our memory – that is, our lifelong accumulation, however valuable and indispensable much of it is to our daily living – gets in the way of our having a deeper, more direct, richer and more peaceful experience of life in each moment ... and most critically in *seeing* Possibility.

Personal discovery from within our mind is the way to transformation and renewal.

DELVING INTO THE UNKNOWN, NOT ACCUMULATING MORE INFORMATION FROM THE KNOWN, IS THE WAY TO OUR TRANSFORMATION

If the answers lie within, personal discovery is an inside-out process. Relying on a counsellor/coach to convey words of wisdom in the hope they will have a lasting impact on the client is less fruitful than being asked questions that evoke personal reflection and insight from a deeper intelligence/reality within, The Realm we call Possibility.

In light of our understanding of fresh Thought, we acknowledge the nature of quiet reflection as leading to inner stillness and insight. This process requires an approach that encourages reflection: being still and being willing to wait patiently in the unknown.

At the heart of The Realm of Possibility Workshop (see Appendix 2) is the acknowledgment that the place of our transformation lies within each of us. The classroom, as it were, is our mind, and the educator is the wellspring of original Thought and our experience of *seeing* Possibility.

QUESTIONING VS TEACHING

History is replete with examples showing that the pivotal element enabling the individual to *see* the nature of fresh Thought and Possibility lies within them.

Vertical inquiry leads us to *see* beyond our memory, beyond our beliefs, opinions, judgements and current understanding of how our life works and why we experience our life the way we do.

The intention behind each question is to lead us away from our story and to explore the unknown world within.

In life, it is necessary to possess all sorts of knowledge and have that knowledge on tap, but we put to you, as we do in this guide, that when such knowledge is on top, it blocks us from *seeing* Possibility. Seeing life through the veil of yesterday is the cause of the problems we face but fail to *see*.

INSIDE-OUT VS OUTSIDE-IN

Life can insist that we question how clearly we see or *see* ourselves and our relationships. In these moments, we are often sorely tested. Our decision appears to be whether to rely on what we see from our conditioned mind, and react and thus struggle with life – to fight with a world that seems to threaten or upset what we are sure is 'the truth of the matter'. Or, we can face these moments with a mind that is understanding, looking towards the unknown, waiting for the insight, the wisdom and the common sense to touch us gently as we stand in silence, open and willing to *see* our world anew.

Personal insights and accessing our innate potential for transformation are seldom, if ever, found in grappling with the content of our thinking – forever a reflection of how we see or *see* life.

It is when faced with questions that have us quietly examining our unaddressed assumptions about life that we *see* the power they have over us and the fallacies in our beliefs, opinions, judgements and knowledge. At those moments, if our mind is quiet enough, we *see* beyond the known into The Realm of Possibility and our transformation.

Vertical inquiry facilitates us in examining our long-held perceptions, raising the chances of our *seeing* Possibility, experiencing life anew from that deeper place of understanding – that place before the existence of our memory.

In much traditional teaching theory, there is the idea that a student learns by listening, looking, reading, experiencing, or by other outside-in ways and then memorising that data. The teacher consolidates the lesson, synthesises the material or puts it together in new ways, which hopefully is *seen* via the creative process that lies within the student.

There is an internal creative process, but the evidence suggests that the method of teaching the synthesising and the creative process does not occur as often as it might with the various outside-in teaching or coaching methods.

What happens, more often than not, is an accumulation of more information, called knowledge, which in and of itself does not lead to discovery, real understanding, transformation of the mind, and renewal. This is why:

- Many experience a quiet mind, inspiration and peace in the presence of their counsellor/coach/mentor, but struggle when they are elsewhere.

- Many, while in a training program, experience the same and *see* life more positively, but soon after leaving that environment, they slip back into their old, less life-affirming habits of thinking, feeling and acting.

- Many, while on a personal-development retreat or attending a self-help group, think, feel and act in a constructive, life-affirming way. On returning to their regular life and work, they slip back into thinking, feeling and behaving as they have for most of their life – in a much less constructive and life-affirming way.

- Without an understanding of what is occurring in our mind – that is, experiencing The Realm of Possibility – we imagine that our experience has to do with our teacher, or we make up a story to explain why we have the experience, a story that attributes meaning to an external source.

Gaining a so-called intellectual understanding of Possibility and impossibility is not a transformative experience that generates the rebirth or renewal of the student.

Our need is to *see* beyond the already known. We need questions that stretch us and require us to *see* beyond our present level of understanding (awareness/consciousness). The process of vertical inquiry paves the way, via this reflection, to insight.

Following an *insight*, we can subsequently benefit from some limited teaching, but reconfirmation and the fleshing-out of the particular *insight* is best gained from our own further *insights* and personal *revelations*. Moreover, this confirmation includes being reminded that all the answers we seek are found within – not from our teacher.

It is the quality of our *insights*, and this alone, that leads to transformation, not the brilliance of the counsellor's teaching or the depth of their understanding.

THE VERTICAL QUESTION AS A SIGNPOST

A vertical question is any question that directs attention away from us, the teacher, and towards the individual's inner wisdom, understanding and innate common sense. After all, the value of a signpost lies in directing attention towards the destination. A vertical question evokes reflection in the individual, rather than an automatic or conditioned response from memory.

As said, it has us examining our unexplored assumptions about life. It is a question that assists in the process of helping us to *see* that we are the thinker and therefore the creator of our experience, and it leads us towards the nature of fresh Thought and Possibility. It plumbs the depths of our inherent understanding by releasing us from our conditioning and exploring our innate nature. From that realm of the unknown, original ideas emerge – novel ways of looking at old problems, new perspectives on long-held beliefs, a more life-enhancing reality.

Is there a risk of putting people into an analytical state with questions, rather than a reflective state? Yes. If a question draws on our memory, we will go into analysing, figuring out, and then back into circular thinking (unless the individual is already awake to what they are doing). If, on the other hand, a question evokes reflection, it will take us towards the unknown and The Realm of Possibility and *seeing* something new or experiencing a fresh take on something old.

When we are sick of sifting through the content of our memory, of endlessly raking over the coals (for some of us, our hell on Earth), vertical questions can unlock the gates to our psychological freedom and connect us with our natural health. That occurs when we *see* that we are creating our experience, moment-to-moment, via Thought. Coupled with that, we become acutely aware of the quality of our in-the-moment thinking.

Here is an example of a dialogue between me ('JW') and a fictitious client ('KS') that uses vertical inquiry effectively:

> JW – 'Kevin, you say you don't understand what I mean by vertical inquiry.'
> KS – 'Yes, I don't get it.'
> JW – 'What is it specifically about that term that you don't get?'
> KS – 'I don't get what you mean by the words "vertical" and "inquiry" put together in that way. It's confusing.'
> JW – 'OK. Do you mind if I ask you a few questions?'
> KS – 'No. Go ahead.'
> JW – 'What does vertical mean to you?'
> KS – 'It means going straight up – going vertically.'
> JW – 'That's what it means to me as well. And I know you understand what inquiry means, so what might vertical inquiry suggest?'
> KS – 'It would suggest a line of inquiry that goes up, straight up; but that doesn't make sense. Up where?'
> JW – 'Yes. Good question. So, if we make an inquiry that takes a person's thinking up – where won't it be taking that person's thinking?'
> KS – 'Well, it certainly won't be down.'
> JW – 'Yes. And where else won't it be taking that person's thinking?'
> KS – 'I guess it won't be going sideways or off at a tangent.'
> JW – 'Right, Kevin: straight up. Not down, not sideways or at a tangent. What does "up" mean to you?'
> KS – 'It means higher rather than lower.'
> JW – 'Yes. Higher than what, Kevin?'
> KS – 'I'm not sure, but right now it seems like a higher, clearer understanding of whatever we are inquiring into. Like me understanding what is meant by the words "vertical inquiry".'

JW – 'You've got it, Kevin. It means questions that take the person questioned, as well as the questioner, to a higher or better understanding of what the person already knows but either hasn't recognised yet or has forgotten.'

You can see from this example that the questions keep drilling into Kevin's unknown or unrecognised understanding. Each answer he comes up with calls for another question, then another, until Kevin discovers the answer to what he thought he didn't know.

Of course, with a real client, what the client is not understanding is more central to their life, their work, sense of wellbeing and peace of mind. However, the process is the same, and the results can be life-changing for them.

THE ROLE OF REFLECTION

Reflection occurs when we become the conscious witness to what we are thinking in the moving moment – observing our thoughts and feelings with curiosity and maybe with wonder. It is occurring when we notice what is going on in our mind without judgement, even when we are judging ourselves for judging ourselves.

Reflection is recognising *that* we are thinking and simultaneously noticing *what* we are thinking. It is being aware of what is passing through our mind – being awake to our creation, our Thought-created reality.

Reflection is a state where we, as the thinker, start to transcend the limitations of our present worldview via *insight*.

Reflection leads us to become aware of the restrictions and limitations of our memory, of our conditioning, of our habitual, analytic, hidebound patterns, i.e. the content of our learned, personalised thinking.

Reflection is the inner gaze by the individual on the known while holding gently the intention of *seeing* the yet-to-be-*seen*, the previously unknown.

Reflection ensues from the process of vertical inquiry, acting as the doorway to *insight*, Possibility and transformation.

INSIGHT: A MOMENT OF POSSIBILITY

Insight is *seeing* in our mind's eye something brand-new, or something in a way we have not recognised before or been aware of until that moment. However, whatever it is we *see*, it comes to us in a context of kindness, understanding, wisdom and common sense.

Insight is waking up from our ignorance.

Insight is the moment of an enriching, possibly exhilarating discovery, one that might transform our work, our life – maybe forever.

Insight is the unforgettable moment experienced by the scientist making a breakthrough; the composer *hearing* the new notes of a beautiful ballad; the sports star, with time seemingly standing still, scoring the winning point in the dying seconds of the game; the entrepreneur *seeing* a revolutionary idea; or the person who, in a moment of kindness, understanding, wisdom and common sense, forgives another human being after years of blaming and anger.

Insight is the gateway to transforming our relationship with the world.

THE LINKS JOINING VERTICAL INQUIRY, REFLECTION AND *INSIGHT*

Vertical inquiry, reflection and *insight* have a lot in common.

Vertical inquiry leads us to the moment where we set aside our world of memory, of seeing life through the illusions of our past.

Vertical inquiry takes us to the point of willingly *not* knowing and having the *intention* to wait in that unknown.

Vertical inquiry, without us realising, moves our gaze from our very personalised thinking towards what we can only describe as impersonal (or arm's-length) thinking.

Vertical inquiry invites us to pause and become reflective on even our most mundane assumptions about how life is for us or how it is for others.

Reflection is, therefore, a natural progression from vertical inquiry.

Reflection enables the individual to *see* that their thinking alone has kept them trapped in a worldview that is restricting their happiness and growth.

Reflection allows freedom from ruminating in analytical thinking.

Reflection leads to a quiet mind, allowing the individual to *see* that they think and that their thinking can shift. This awareness encourages further reflection.

IN SUMMARY

It is from the quiet, unbounded space of reflection that *insights* arise. Those *insights* will inspire in the counsellor/coach fresh vertical inquiry, as it will in the client. That, in turn, will lead to deeper reflection and further *insights for both*.

The continuing cycle of vertical inquiry/reflection/*insight* serves to deepen our understanding of how we have constructed our life and relationships, and how we might discover renewal via fresh Thought and Possibility.

Vertical inquiry, in my experience, is the best way to spark personal *insights* that will provide a sound and continuing basis for lasting transformation. This view is based on at least two criteria:

- The degree to which the client transforms in a way that their life and relationships are, without exception, happier and more fulfilling.
- The degree to which the movement lasts over time and holds up in the face of life's vagaries.

In our experience, tapping the wisdom, common sense and natural healthy functioning (The Realm of Possibility) that already exist in every individual seems to be achieved most effectively and efficiently by directing the individual towards *seeing* the inside-out creation of life, via vertical inquiry.

Please join me in a Realm of Possibility Workshop (see Appendix 2).

CHAPTER 7

A CHECKLIST FOR YOUR BUSINESS OR ORGANISATION – TO SHOW HOW POSSIBILITY CAN HELP

Keep asking yourself the right questions, and you'll find the right answer. Or, find someone who can ask you those questions that take you into the previously unseen.

Use the checklist below to assess the prevailing state of your business or organisation. I strongly encourage you to consider your own state of mind first.

- Do you have a clearly enunciated promise that you want to deliver to your clients, patients, those in your care, those that work for you or those for whom you work?
- Do most individuals take 100-percent responsibility for delivering the organisation's promise – stated or implied?
- Or is delivering the organisation's promise hit-and-miss?
- Do most understand what 'delivering the promise' means?
- Is moving the organisation forward like wading through molasses?
- Is making a decent profit (return on investment) like a mission impossible?
- Are market conditions and shifts in them *seen* and experienced as an opportunity and responded to, or seen as a problem that conjures fear?

A Checklist for your Business or Organisation – to show how Possibility can help

- Are conditions either not *seen*, or maybe seen and experienced as a problem too big to deal with, or simply deemed irrelevant?
- Are stress, anxiety and worry common?
- Is staff turnover high?
- Does your organisation have high absenteeism?
- Do your people have irregular work patterns?
- Is alcohol abuse or drug-taking a problem?
- Do you have productivity or performance difficulties that go unaddressed?
- Is 'passing the buck' or shifting the burden of responsibility to others commonplace?
- Are market conditions (downturns, interest rates, lenders' demands, competitor discounting, the government, world conditions) used as a reason for the poor performance of the organisation?
- Is a lack of follow-up and follow-through a problem?
- What is the level of initiative, creative-idea generation and the quality of business development within the organisation?
- Are conversions from enquiries to doing business a problem?
- Are customer-service standards low?
- Is customer loyalty a thing of the past?
- Is there cooperation between individuals, departments, branches, divisions?
- Is the quality of your product or service down on what it needs to be?
- Do workers feel they can achieve a seamless work and family life to enable them to contribute more effectively to both?
- Is there a working environment for creating a healthier workplace in your company?
- Is there a high level of vitality and wellbeing in your organisation?
- Above all else, is your business or organisation providing goods and services that are sustainable and serving the common good?

No matter what your position, from very junior to chairman of the board, understanding the Fourth Element is what enables you to facilitate the development of yourself and simultaneously contribute to realising the potential of the organisation as a whole.

As explored throughout this guide, *seeing* Possibility is exhilarating and never fails to contribute to all involved.

FINALLY

*'The master of the art of living makes little distinction between his
work and his play,
his labour and his leisure,
his mind and his body, his education and his recreation,
his love and his religion. He hardly knows which is which;
he simply pursues his vision of excellence in whatever
he does, leaving others to decide whether he is working
or playing. To him he is always doing both.'*

BUDDHA

Possibility is *awareness* lighting our way forward on whatever path we may find ourselves. For those willing to surrender to the mysterious universal energy manifesting as Thought in our mind, Possibility awaits.

In that state I *see* a world in which you and I live from Possibility – a world in which we are kind and understanding of one another. Where wisdom, common sense, and a sense of fairness and decency govern all our decisions at work and at play. Where our actions regarding the planet and all that live on, below or above her are sustainable and taken with the common good foremost in mind.

We have a decision to make: whether we live lost in the illusion of 'The Game of Living' and 'The Business Game', refusing to recognise that our experience is the creation of our capacity to think, nothing more and nothing less. Or we can play 'The Game of Living' and 'The Business Game' *consciously and in union with Life* and all its manifestations.

I hope you will join me on that journey ... John

APPENDIX 1

POSSIBILITY IS NOT IDEALISM

'Idealist: a cynic in the making.'

Irving Layton

Two states of mind are always available to us from which to see – or *see* – the world.

In one sense, the *difference* between them is simple semantics; however, there is a deeper reality that takes us from the realm of ideals and idealism to the realm of action. Idealism is another word for the theory-rich but Possibility-poor way we can be in the world. Therefore, exploring the concept of the idealist is one way to reflect on what keeps us from living our idealist thinking.

Ideals have been stumbling blocks along my own journey! I used to pat myself on the back for how good and worthwhile my ideals were. I was all about social justice, worker participation, conservation, peace, equality of opportunity, living and working in harmony, being a loving neighbour, an enlightened boss, a loving husband and father, living an honourable life.

The bare facts were that these ideals mostly – in some cases, always – didn't coincide with the way I lived my life, and often still don't. I am not suggesting these are bad ideals. I just did not understand life from the vantage point of Possibility, although I did visit that realm and *saw* fresh ideas, a new way of looking at life. But these often became simply additional ideals in the process.

And, like every human being, I was doing the absolute best I could with my lack of understanding of how we see or *see* the world. I hadn't *seen* that our professed philosophy of everyday living often wasn't what we said it was. Nor was it what we wanted it to be; what we intended it to be; what we believed it to be.

No. Our philosophy of everyday living is actually how we *act*, how we actually live, behave and relate to each other and to the environment in each moment of each day. That alone reflects accurately our true philosophy.

Our philosophy is not what we say it is. Our philosophy is the way we live out each day. The ideal of how I wanted to live my life (and how I wanted the world to be) might have been everything I wanted it to be in my mind, but it was not how it was in my life. In my own mind, I was a legend.

Like so many idealists before me, I had been living in the realm of high-minded but self-defeating knowledge, beliefs, opinions and judgements – the state of mind that precludes ideals coming to fruition and being our lived reality. I didn't recognise that I was trapped in my conditioning, let alone how to intentionally *see* through that unseen web of belief and into the realm of Possibility, and be free to live the ideals I claimed to cherish.

I recall being in a training workshop in Boston in the early 1990s. Dr George Pransky, a prominent Possibility trainer, was leading the session.

George posed a question to me. I was fair game. What follows is my best representation of what occurred. Remember, our memories are most unreliable, exponentially so of events that occurred over 25 years earlier. The exchange is also a beautiful example of 'vertical questioning'.

> 'John,' George said to me, 'what is your philosophy of life?'
> Confidently, and with a little false pride, I responded, 'George, that's simple – to be a loving human being.'
> 'That's very good – very noble, and quite wonderful,' he replied. 'But are you?' he asked.
> 'I really try to be,' I replied.
> 'I didn't ask if you try to be, John. I asked, are you a loving human being?'
> 'I do my absolute best.'
> 'Now, John, I don't want to be difficult, but I didn't ask you if you do your best to be a loving human being. I asked you whether you are a loving human being.'
> 'I really work at being a loving human being. I really do, George,' I said with growing bewilderment.
> 'Come on, John, my question wasn't whether you do your best at being a loving human being. My question was: are you a loving human being?'
> 'George, I can't make it any clearer,' I shot back, now with a tinge of annoyance. 'I work on being a loving human being each and every day. I am dedicated to being a loving human being.'

'Gee, John,' George came back, 'I get that you work on it and are dedicated to it, but that is not what I asked you. I asked: are you a loving human being?'

I will go no further with our dialogue. It went on till the morning break. That was a long time. George kept asking the same question and I managed to continue to miss his point. How I managed to keep answering with a different twist each time and so avoid *seeing* the deeper point was testimony to the fact that I was lost in idealism and removed from *what is*. I didn't *see* that saying you are something, i.e. that I *am* a loving human being, and actually *being* a loving human being are not the same thing.

We went to the morning tea break with me feeling very lost and frustrated. What was interesting was that, while I missed the point, it was clear that each of the other males (apart from me, they all had PhDs) missed it too. But all the women got it straight away.

While drowning my sorrows in a cuppa during the break, the penny finally dropped. I had an *insight*. What we say our philosophy is, is not what it is. How we live our life is our philosophy. This also shows that the results from vertical questioning are not always immediate.

There is our ideal, our vision of how we would like to be, how we try to be, etc. Our philosophy, on the other hand, is where the rubber meets the road. It is the way we live our life, each and every day.

What an important breakthrough for me that was! I saw how deluded I was about how I was in the world. I was not how I 'believed myself to be'. I was how I 'behaved'.

I would spike into the realm of fresh Thought and *see* Possibility, but those wonderful moments of clarity, beautiful thoughts, feelings and discovery were not understood by me for what they were. Then, as now, I was unfolding. The difference today is that I have at least a clue as to what is going on in my mind. Today I say the vision I hold for my life is 'to be a loving human being'. That keeps me on track most of the time to be one.

Being an idealist is to be lost in the desire that things be other than how we are creating them. As idealists, we want life to be the theory we have constructed in our heads. And not the reality we live. We don't realise that everything in each moment is the perfect launching pad into Possibility and living the ideal. In that state, we're naturally tuned to kindness, understanding, wisdom and common sense. We're actually living what we'd call an ideal.

Life as it is for each of us (including that we may be an idealist) is absolutely okay. Our job isn't to direct life in one way or another, it is to *see* life free of the contamination of our ideals and to be free to be who we really are – embodiments of kindness, understanding, wisdom and common sense – and to live responsibly and sustainably.

These two states of mind – one the realm of believing in theoretical ideals, the other of living our ideals – feel profoundly different. Our behaviour and effectiveness are equally different in these two states. If we're an idealist, we remain unfulfilled, no matter how hard we work towards achieving our ideals, how many protest marches we walk, how much we talk, write, philosophise and try to influence. We feel unfulfilled no matter how famous and celebrated we may be; our work and our satisfaction with it will be a shadow of what it might be if fuelled by Possibility and being our ideals.

In reality, idealism is the antithesis of actually living the imagined ideal. Manifesting the ideal is the only thing that really makes a difference in our life, our relationships or in our world.

Think of the man or woman who sincerely wants a loving relationship with their partner, or even the one who is genuinely earnest about living from a loving state – but in both cases they fail to live their ideal. He or she may read or even write books on the subject, attend courses, participate in relationship counselling and even, as in my case, counsel and coach others on how to have a loving relationship. The entire focus of their life may be on loving relationships, but their day-to-day reality is the only thing that counts. If they behave in unloving ways in their relationships, their 'ideal' of having loving relationships is but a figment of their imagination.

A simple way to look at this is that what we *do* is our actual philosophy. What we *say* is our ideal.

What causes the difference? Don't look at whether you 'go' to church, but instead look carefully at how kindly you live your life. Do you 'turn the other cheek'?

Don't look at whether you're a peace activist. Look rather at whether your relationships, particularly those with people you don't much like or respect, are kind and peaceful. Don't look at whether you're a climate-change activist; look at your lifestyle and your own greenhouse gas emissions.

The '-isms' put forward over the centuries to save humanity from its erroneous thinking, feelings and behaviour haven't worked. Why is that?

Idealists would say a particular ideal (Christianity, Islam, communism, capitalism …) hasn't worked simply because it wasn't given sufficient opportunity, wasn't sufficiently understood or funded, or people weren't dedicated enough to bring the ideal to realisation. But whether it is religious, philosophical, psychological, sociological, political, economic, ethical or spiritual idealism, each has failed to create a society that walks gently hand-in-hand with the wonder of Life. Each has failed to bring about a world community living in a state of kindness, understanding, wisdom and common sense; one that lives and shares the fruits of Possibility.

Idealism purports to be about creating something better, something new, but is actually a linear movement (looking for change) that transports, via our conditioned mind, the past into the future.

So what can create a spike in our awareness, a quantum leap into a new reality? How can we go from idealising to being? How can we act in a loving, understanding, wise, common-sense way and be the catalyst for transformation in our own lives?

What is the key to unlocking the way to our transformation, and to unlocking the shackles of idealism and *seeing* that which already exists within our mind before the addition of ideals – before that conditioned realm that harbours our beliefs, opinions, judgements and knowledge? How do we quit talking about what we want to do, what we aspire to do – and actually do it, be it?

The answer lies in understanding and *seeing* within our mind's eye how the human experience is created, how we create our reality in each moment. Understand this, and we are freed from the trap of idealism. We shift to a life lived increasingly in a context of kindness, understanding, wisdom and common sense – a life of action and rationality rather than one of self-righteousness and pomposity about our great and noble ideals.

And to *see* to the heart of this is to awaken to the factors that give shape and substance to all human experience. These factors create personal reality for you, for me and for everyone on Earth. Just as gravity is the force of attraction between particles and mass in our universe, so too are these factors the force behind creating the human condition, for better or worse.

As detailed throughout this guide:

- Factor One is Thought, the formless energy with which we *see* and manifest original, fresh, clear and creative thinking in the moment (the realm of Possibility.) And it's that same energy with which we see life reconstructed from our memory, re-creating our past experience, conditioning and knowledge in the moment (the state described as impossibility).

- Factor Two is consciousness or awareness. Awareness is our *seeing* that we create the totality of our experience of our life (our personal reality) via Thought in one of two forms: one, as original, impersonal thinking from the fountain of fresh Thought and Possibility; two, as recycled, personal thinking re-created from our memory, the latter being the realm of impossibility and the home of our idealism (our beliefs).

So long as we strive for and profess our ideals (as I do in this guide, for example), we are most likely and quite innocently re-creating the past and failing to live the ideal as our moment-to-moment reality.

To be aware is to be awake to the fact that our ideal might be:

- a wonderful notion, but in reality is just a theory in our mind;
- what we are thinking about, talking about, striving for, but not what we are actually living in each moment as our way of life.

Consequently, any ideal simply held in our memory and talked about as a good or even a grand idea is just that, and can prevent us from manifesting the ideal as part of our living reality. Why? Because being present to *what is*, is a state of Possibility, the *being* state of all ideals. On the other hand, living from our memories is being lost in our lifeless past and simply represents our rhetoric, not our lived philosophy.

Those old sayings, which go something like, 'He is an armchair: environmentalist, social-justice advocate, healthy living advocate', etc. describe the idealist – great on theory but lacking in practice. 'Do as I say, not as I do' is another way of describing the idealist.

Ideals will be out of our reach so long as we reach for them, talk about them, write about them – rather than live them in that state of actually *being* our philosophy.

The trap of idealism is wrapped up in the phrase, 'talking the talk, not walking the walk'.

LIVING FROM IDEALISM OR IN POSSIBILITY

The trap for idealists is that believing ourselves
to be one prevents us living the ideal.

Following are examples of the gulf between living in the realm of idealism (the realm of good or great ideas) and the realm of Possibility (the realm of kindness, understanding, wise and common-sense action):

A person living in Idealism	A person living in Possibility
wants and promotes peace	lives in peace
wants intimacy and closeness with partner	is intimate and close with partner
wants a loving relationship	is loving in relationship
dedicates their life to expressing or writing about their philosophical perspectives	lives their philosophy – in kindness, understanding, wisdom and common sense
wants communication	is communicative
believes listening to others is crucial, even teaches the art of deep listening	listens deeply to others and, as importantly, to self
advocates the virtue of forgiveness	forgives unconditionally
preaches tolerance and acceptance	embraces all of humanity – no exceptions
judges self's and others' shortcomings in not measuring up to their ideals (however innocent the judgement)	sees the fundamental innocence in self and others
advocates loyalty	is loyal
espouses that we should do what is in the interest of the common good	acts in ways that support the common good
professes the importance of being understanding	is understanding
teaches the ideal	lives the ideal
seeks enlightenment	is at peace with being unenlightened
believes spirituality is divine, special, exclusive, or must be earned and is for the special or chosen few	sees spirituality in everything; as being all-inclusive, ordinary; from the cesspit to the rainforest, psychopath to saint
promotes generosity	is generous
teaches the virtue of honesty	does not consider the alternative
fosters the importance of gratitude	feels grateful
preaches (i.e. from the Bible, Koran, Kabbalah or Bhagavad Gita)	lives from a state of kindness, understanding, wisdom and common sense
believes the end justifies the means	*sees* that the means is the end
isdom and common ses th	

In the moment we *see* the illusion of our own beliefs, we *see* our idealism as being one of well-intentioned good ideas but yet to be our lived reality.

We *see* that we are missing this moment, the only moment there is, to live beyond the idea of the ideal and experience kindness, understanding, wisdom and common sense.

In that instant, we are present to *what is*, without any desire for it to be consistent with our imagined ideals. To *see what is*, is to *see* through the illusion of memory and *see* free of knowledge, opinion, belief or judgement. It's to *see* into the realm of Possibility and the wonder of Life.

Idealism, in all its forms, is what creates separation from once-loving relationships.

It is, in the main, driving all movements and divides society into proponents of various ideals.

Idealism is behind peace activists fighting with mounted police and spilling blood by poking sharpened sticks into the flanks of their horses; it's behind the idealisation of 'God' as justification for terrorist bombings and beheadings.

It's at the heart of the bitterness of the pro-abortion and pro-life debate. It's why we are upset with what we see every news hour and read in the morning papers.

SO, FELLOW IDEALISTS, WHAT DO WE NEED TO UNDERSTAND?

Ideals live in our imagination but are actioned by the power of Possibility.

In understanding Thought (that formless energy generating our life and experience) we *see* that we can recycle past memories and thus create an idealised reality, or we can access fresh Thought and experience a reality that is present to life as it is ... not as we imagine it to be or should be.

What we need to understand is that when we experience fresh Thought, we *see* Possibility and experience a feeling of connectedness, peace and good humour.

In that state of awareness we *see* our idealism for what it was – simply a good idea separating us from the deeper reality of living a life of action inspired by Possibility. We *see* into a reality free of fear – a reality that is open to Life as it is – and in response to this we take the action we are moved to take.

To experience life beyond enslavement to our conditioning – to our beliefs, opinions and judgements – is to be free. Free to get a fresh start. Free to take action without fear or favour. Free to embrace life unconditionally.

The primrose path of idealism is *seen* for what it is: the illusion in which you and I imagine ourselves to live – but don't. The source of our transformation exists beyond idealism. It is *seeing what is*. It is *seeing* Possibility.

APPENDIX 2

THE REALM OF POSSIBILITY WORKSHOP: A (NOT-FOR-PROFIT) PRIMER FOR A CREATIVE LIFE

Transforming yourself transforms your organisation.

The Possibility Workshop is offered to anyone who, having read this guide, is interested in participating in a three-day workshop to further explore the power of Possibility.

We are creating our personal reality every moment and forming a continuous and ever-moving and evolving reality. You are doing it right now. Think about that ...

Change the wording a little: our reality is what we create, moment by moment, from the gift of Thought. Our world is what we are thinking and feeling right now; it is uniquely ours.

No matter how hard I try, I cannot create your world – your organisation. I can try to influence it. I can try to help you think and feel differently about it – but in no way at all can I change or create your reality. I cannot change the way you think and feel about life. The way you think about life is the way life is for you in each unfolding moment. It is your potential and your momentary state of Possibility or impossibility.

When we wake up to the simple but profound reality that 'we think into existence our reality', we experience a shift in consciousness that has us more aware and more alive than ever before. There's nothing mystical here. It's simply a shift in our *awareness* – us operating with greater clarity, greater *insight*, and at that new level, perhaps for the first time. It is us *seeing what is*!

The deliciousness of creating freshness is experienced in moments when we *see* our partners, our children and grandchildren, our friends, our colleagues, our clients, everyone as if for the first time. The illusion of our memories, expectations, history and bias (one way or the other) is what hides them from us and blocks us from *seeing* who they really are, in each new, fresh moment.

When we hold ourselves and others responsible for life being the way it is – when we look to upbringing, environment, past mistakes or experiences – we are lost in our story. And we are blinded to our deeper reality of Possibility. Re-creating our experience in each moment from our lifelong accumulation of ideas as to why life is the way it is, and others are the way they are, is seeing life from a state of impossibility. It is our unrecognised rationale for the way life is.

We are busy using our past experiences to make sense of our life and put it in the order we believe it should be in, and when we do that we simply continue to live out our story – our beliefs, opinions, judgements and knowledge – nothing more, nothing less. Nothing changes. We are simply projecting our past forward into our future. Reasons and rationales, however compelling, are figments of our imagination. They are the story we have methodically or haphazardly created to try to make sense of our momentary experience, which we call our life.

Once we *see* Possibility, we *see* people like you and me who have learned habits, habits that could be described as unrecognised disabilities. I say disabilities because we don't *see* that they are self-created boundaries to fresh discovery, creativity, direct action and a deeper understanding of our true self … our loving nature.

We need not accept that we must remain as we believe our conditioning, gender, or culture has shaped us. On this journey of discovery, we must first acquire an understanding: that we already possess a deeper intelligence beyond the limitations of our memory, beyond everything about which we deceive ourselves, beyond believing that life is what we believed it to be.

Do we want to remain a prisoner of a finite past? Or would we rather *see* and experience the wonderful world of infinite Possibility? It's just a thought away.

COST AND DURATION

The Workshop/Retreat is offered by The Realm of Possibility Project Foundation. As the Foundation is not-for-profit, the costs are set to cover our expenses and to contribute a small amount to our operations. Costs vary somewhat depending on the venue and whether accommodation is provided. We encourage participants to stay at the venue if possible. The three-day program usually runs from Friday afternoon to Sunday afternoon.

THE PROJECT'S AIM

The Workshop's aim is to assist all participants (including the facilitator) to *see* Possibility and thus create a fresh, sustainable future for themselves. Whereas this written guide has lots of abstraction in it, the Workshop is relentlessly practical and experiential. You'll be exploring Possibility in the company of a group of fellow explorers. It is made available for those looking for the doorway through which to step.

The specific aim over the three days is transformation. The aim is for you to leave with a deeper experience of Possibility, or perhaps a conscious experience of Possibility for the first time. At the very least, you will come away:

- as a deeper listener to yourself and others, listening to life with greater clarity and heeding what you hear in a heightened state of awareness;

- with more understanding of yourself and therefore of others and, consequently, a stronger feeling of kindness and understanding and a heightened level of wisdom and common sense;

- better able to make a loving difference in your relationships by being present and available;

- better prepared, by your presence, to bring others together in a way that nurtures their spirit and helps open their hearts and minds to Possibility;

- as a wiser woman walking down the street or a more understanding man standing in line at the checkout;

- being the leader the world desperately needs at this time in history.

WHO IS IT FOR?

We welcome the participation of individuals who are interested in *seeing* Possibility, not only for themselves but for society and humanity as a whole. It may be that you want to *see* a way to achieving:

- a fairer, kinder and more just workplace;

- a transformation from a society dominated by power and control leadership to one that values a true blend of freedom of expression and human decency;
- increasing numbers of entrepreneurs creating employment and thus less dependence on taxpayer-funded welfare subsidies;
- a naturally occurring and sustainable redistribution of wealth from a growing minority to an increasing majority;
- workplaces that are fun, fulfilling and financially rewarding for employers and employees alike.

It's for those who personally want to move from a consumption-driven, credit-based, increasingly debt-dependent, seemingly never-satisfied materialistic lifestyle to one featuring greater simplicity, sustainability and inclusion.

- It might be for those who want to step off the treadmill without being killed financially.
- It might be for those who want to *see*:
    - their children and grandchildren living in a world at peace with itself;
    - world religions congruent with what their founder *saw* – a world of kindness, understanding, wisdom and common sense, not divisiveness and separation;
    - a quickening towards environmental sustainability;
    - politicians in service to their constituents rather than themselves and narrow interests;
    - sustainable agricultural practices, adequate food supplies globally, and food and water that are poison-free;
    - schools as places of discovery, liberty and Possibility rather than houses of robotic learning, restraint and narrow, ideology-based thinking;
    - universities as places that encourage free thinkers, free thinking and Possibility, independent of global corporations pushing their particular financial interests, and independent of ideological and political correctness from the left, right or centre;

- o businesses that want to be profitable – not at the expense of the community or the environment, but as vital contributors to the health, wealth and wellbeing of all.
- It might be for people with a social conscience who want to be powerful, peaceful vanguards and who want to be able to clarify their thinking and thus their purpose and take action, who want to transform from being prisoners of problematic thinking to becoming architects of sustainable solutions.
- It might be for farmers, market gardeners, doctors, lawyers, teachers, plumbers, carpenters, mechanics, and people from every walk of life who want to create a wholesome, decent community.
- It's certainly for those who want and are willing to take responsibility and be accountable for every nook and cranny of their life.
- It's certainly for those who want to take the power back from the illusory 'them' and who want to live in a society that understands that we (you and I) are 100-percent responsible for creating crime, unemployment and homelessness. That we are responsible for the marginalised and disadvantaged, the degradation and pollution of the environment, the taxpayer subsidies for unsustainable commercial practices and growing welfare dependency, the full jails and overflowing surgeries and hospitals.
- It's certainly for those who see that they are 100-percent responsible for what is happening right now and *see* Possibility in creating a new future, a just, sustainable, kind, welcoming, hospitable, inclusive, more fun-filled society.
- It's certainly for those that are willing to turn their thinking upside-down and inside-out and recognise that, for better or worse, we are the creators of what we see and the reality we experience and that, for better or worse, we either see from impossibility or *see* from Possibility.
- It's for those who understand that we don't have to fix 'them' but simply wake up to what we have created, and re-create our own transformed future.
- It's for anyone willing to break out of their trance and *see* that '*we*' are 'them'. And that we can transform our life, families, workplaces, neighbourhoods, country, and the world.

- It's for people who want to reclaim their streets, neighbourhoods, suburbs and cities.

- It's for people who already understand that the world can be a happier, healthier and more sustainable place for this and future generations.

- It's for people who want to *see* how to be part of the transformation, by letting go of their past to create a future of Possibility.

The Workshop welcomes and encourages the participation of private-sector organisations, government and NGOs.

Your objectives may be to seek:

- a reduction in alcohol and drug use;
- a reduction in domestic violence;
- an increase in homeless people finding accommodation;
- an increase in disadvantaged youth into education and employment;
- an increase in disadvantaged men and women into community;
- more people with disabilities welcomed into advantaged society;
- more Aboriginal people healthy and happy;
- more offenders rehabilitated rather than punished.

OUR APPROACH

Come prepared to engage. Come prepared to discover for yourself what Possibility looks and feels like. There will be limited teaching, lecturing, handouts or discussion, although participants will, upon enrolment, each be given (free of charge) a copy of my other book, *Possibility ... a State of Mind*, a companion volume to this one.

All questions (except those seeking clarification) will more than likely be responded to with a question. You already have all the answers to solve what puzzles you. Our job will be to simply keep pointing you in the direction of your innate connection to Possibility.

These three days will be no armchair ride. We will facilitate the process assuming that you are in self-discovery mode and not looking for more second-hand information. You already have enough of that and it is part of the paralysis-by-analysis information overload that we live in; it's more of the umpteen unread or un-actioned surveys, reports, books and expert analyses.

This Workshop is a time to reclaim your power as an equal among equals, exploring your mind and the unlimited power of Possibility. You will be treated as a respected human being, equal in every respect.

But we have absolutely no idea how these three days will work out, or if a single attendee will *see* authentic Possibility within their mind. We mean that. We offer no guarantees.

WHAT WE *DO* PROMISE

You will be treated as an important guest and our hospitality will include wholesome foods, deliciously prepared. You will not go hungry!

You will not be asked to do anything other than to be part of the larger group and to be with others in small groups. You will not be asked to give more than a five-second introduction of yourself – e.g. 'I'm John Wood from Darlington' – or you can pass on introducing yourself. You will not be asked why you are here or what you want to gain from attending. Each person will be given a name badge with their first name shown.

Our priority is the safety and inclusion of each individual. We will be vigilant throughout the three days to ensure that each person feels safe to explore their inner world at all times.

Listed below are some of the obstructions to *seeing* Possibility, the habits which most of us innocently employ to live our lives. They keep us stuck in our conditioning, in impossibility. For the duration of the workshop, we will ask that you let go of:

- giving advice to anyone on anything, even if asked;
- coaching anyone, even if asked;
- telling parts or all of your story or anyone else's story, even if asked;
- answering for anyone else, even if asked;
- giving the small or large group your opinions, beliefs and judgements, even if asked;
- correcting anything you think, hear or see is out of place, including any breaches of these requests, even if asked;

- taking notes, as doing so is a block to *seeing* Possibility. Remember, this is about *seeing* Possibility, not learning another method.

Any exceptions to the above will be to ensure the safety and wellbeing of each individual.

Each day will be invested in reflecting on a series of questions created to assist you to *see* into the way you think and to *see* into and beyond your answers. There are no right or wrong answers; the answers will be a reflection of each person's separate reality and, we trust, a stepping stone to your *seeing* Possibility. As exploration and self-discovery, rather than 'learning', are the key objectives, we utilise the 'Vertical Inquiry' questioning process in the Workshop (see Chapter 6).

The group will be limited to 30 participants. Fifteen will be required for the process to work and for the group to go ahead.

WHY WE TAKE THE APPROACH WE DO

The distinction between being taught and the self-discovery process we employ is this: 'being taught' is gaining knowledge from another source and is by definition second-hand information. As well informed and important as that information might be, it is another person's discovery. Our aim is for you to make your own discoveries. Knowledge can be gathered about and around Possibility, but the experience of *seeing* Possibility is unlikely to be had from second-hand information.

As I have mentioned in the guide, self-discovery *seen* via original Thought is yours. You own it! You can rightfully claim 100-percent ownership of whatever you find within the clear space of your own mind. It comes from your innate capacity for experiencing original Thought and is yours for life. It is an unshakeable, deep-seated understanding, and – it's still not 'the truth'. Rather, it's the result of you or me *seeing* Possibility at that point in time. There is always and will always be more to *see*.

Please visit our website for information on the next Possibility Workshop. I would love to meet you there ... John

therealmofpossibility.org.au

www.ingramcontent.com/pod-product-compliance
Lightning Source LLC
Chambersburg PA
CBHW020423220526
45464CB00002B/541